The Infinite Sojourns Of Consciousness

<u>Philosophical Fiction</u>

And God said:
"Let them know the truth".

authorHOUSE®

AuthorHouse™
1663 Liberty Drive, Suite 200
Bloomington, IN 47403
www.authorhouse.com
Phone: 1-800-839-8640

First published by AuthorHouse 9/25/2008

ISBN: 978-1-4389-1733-7 (sc)
ISBN: 978-1-4389-1732-0 (hc)

Library of Congress Control Number: 2008908568

Printed in the United States of America
Bloomington, Indiana

This book is printed on acid-free paper.

Dedication

This book is dedicated to my loving wife Joy who is my strength in this physical plane we now feel we exist in.

My three daughters Shawn, Brenda and Kari who also have given me from themselves and their children the joys in this life it is impossible to explain.

To the many dear friends I have been most fortunate to have met on this sojourn, also to the many I have yet to meet.

Bless you all.

Edited by
Kim McDarison
Joy Anderson
Bill Dupuis
Shawn O'Leary

The Infinite Sojourns of Collective Consciousness Individualized.

by

Rev. Kenneth Earl Anderson D.D.

Ken the Carpenter, with help!

Table of Contents

Poems

Short stories

My moment in time!

There is only the Infinite Moment.

That is all one can experience.

The Infinite Moment

When we look at the past we only see what we cannot change.

When we look to the future with hope we are only putting off what can be in this moment.

When we live for this moment to the best of our ability, life can always be good.

The past is gone. The future will never be.

This infinite moment is all you can ever see.

Comments, remarks and observations

Heavens Music
On earth
The sound of Laughter

THE SOUND OF LAUGHTER

I could hear the sound of laughter, I thought everyone could hear. But there were people dying. I could see their loved ones crying; yet the laughter grew louder.

Street fighting and gangs were killing each other as though no one was their brother. The laughter grew louder.

The aged were leaving, would we ever feel their love again? But the beautiful sound of laughter became still louder.

Every few moments there was a murder, and suicide seemed a means to an end. This killing and dying appeared to be an accepted trend.

The laughter became louder. Why?

I didn't know but it made me want to cry.

Accidents and senseless random killing were also a moment-by-moment occurrence. With all of this, how could one give our young any loving assurance? The crescendo of laughter grew increasingly higher. By now when I spoke of love or anything positive I felt to be a liar.

It seemed now that only laughter could be heard, but people were dying everywhere. The good, the bad, it did not discriminate the laughter went on.

I could hear no sobbing, only laughter. Why only laughter? It seemed to be growing louder, or somehow coming closer to me. Was there something I did not know, or could not see?

Suddenly I knew I had died. My mind the conscious,

The sub-conscious and even the super-conscious realized I too had moved to the other side. Could there be a just or true cause?

As the realization and understanding truly became clear there was no right, wrong, unjust or fair.

I smiled, then I started to laugh, I could not stop. I laughed and I laughed then I laughed even harder as I began to understand what the other laughter had been about.

Only now could I see that I had not died, but rather had escaped from the illusion of death and dying. Again I laughed aloud then I looked back at the dear souls still locked in the unreal world of life and death as was seen there.

Suddenly there was no laughter. Where am I? My God. Where am I?

I have awoken. I was only having a dream. Was I? Have I awoken or truly fallen back fast asleep? Then let me awake to the laughter, the Love, and the knowing that all is well in Heaven and on earth. There are no two sides. There is only LIFE with lessons for each to learn.

As I continue with my daily exercises and achieve my unknown goals I will learn better how to love unconditionally and know what I am going through has no rules, except that I will learn the lesson I have come to better understand, that LIFE is LOVE and HAPPINESS, everywhere, all the time.

It is a trip, only a trip. No matter what you may perceive as right or wrong, good or bad. Learn YOUR lesson. To the degree that you learn and understand will designate the next segment of your INFINITE journey.

Do not question of anyone, why? But for you when this class is over you will UNDERSTAND, you did not die.

YOU too WILL ONLY HEAR THE LAUGHTER.

Start laughing now!!!!!

All is good.

Comments, remarks and observations

Comments, remarks and observations

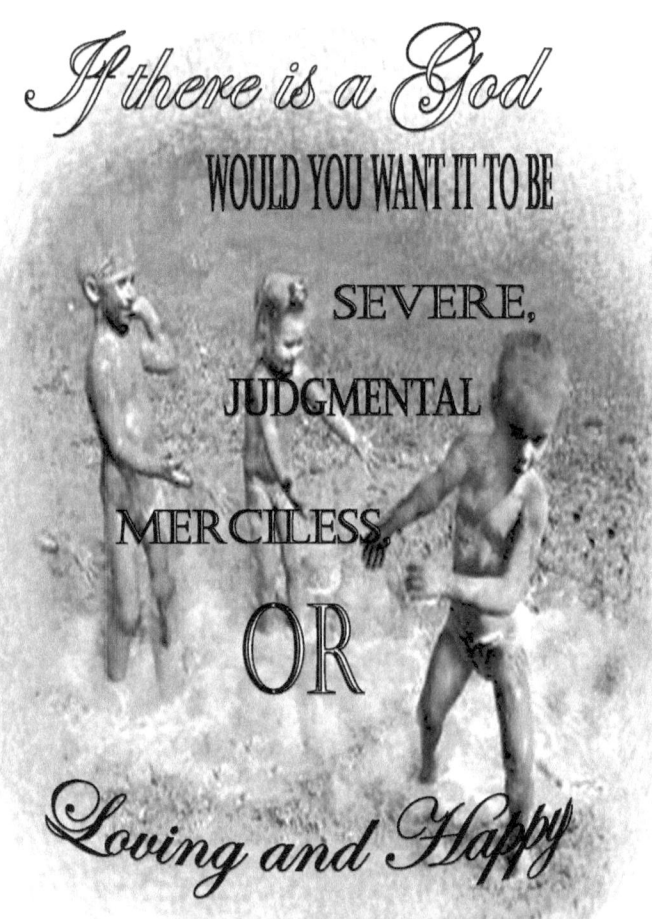

If there is a God
WOULD YOU WANT IT TO BE
SEVERE,
JUDGMENTAL
MERCILESS,
OR
Loving and Happy

A Fun!
Happy!
And
Loving!

God

Caricatures --- <u>God</u>   <u>Gabriel</u>   <u>Michael</u>   <u>Lucifer</u>

Three children who appeared to be between six and eight years of age were playing in a large mud puddle laughing, splashing and throwing mud, with no malice only enjoying their fun.

The laughter was loud and without restriction and all three were caked with the heavy muck.

A beautiful angel slowly descended near where the three were playing.

"God! God! Please God, won't you please come out? I really must talk with you," Lucifer beseeched.

One of the muddiest youngsters stopped and looked around at the apparent distraught angel.

"What is it you want Lucifer?" God asked. "Come on in and have some fun. Lighten up and enjoy your existence as who you are right now. What you do is up to you so why do you worry so much?"

"You are the figurehead of all of Infinite collective consciousness and you're playing in a mud puddle.

What is going to happen with everything if it's not taken care of?" Lucifer asked.

A childish laugh came from the One as he playfully threw a clump of the muck toward Lucifer.

Lucifer raised his wings and gracefully rose above the mucky projectile.

"Gab, Mick. Let's get him to play." God suggested.

A slight glint came into Lucifer's eyes and he quickly left the area.

The three slowly rose above the mud and as it disappeared beneath them, they were again in pure radiantly white robes, sadly watching their loved companion move away.

"Why is he so serious?" Gabriel asked. "He must realize everything we do is created by us, and will change as we change, to whatever we want."

God and Michael looked over at Gabriel, Michael with a concerned look and God with a bright smile.

"What are you smiling about?" Michael queried.

"He'll come around when he realizes how much better life is when lived happily, rather then in such seriousness," God said.

The three disappeared in different directions.

Later, God's secretary announced, "Lucifer is here to see you."

"Good to see you again so soon," God said. "I do love so much staying in contact with all that there is, and you of course are so very important to me and it has been only a few millennia."

"Yes of course you do. Do you remember the last time we saw each other and how you threw mud at me?" Lucifer asked glumly.

"Of course I do Lucifer. What a day that was. We had so much fun I was crying tears," God said.

"Yes of course you were. I too was crying," Lucifer said. "There is nothing like the tears of joy," God replied.

At that point Lucifer said, "God, we need to talk. There are some things I feel should be changed, and it needs to be established now."

"All right," God said. "What are they? I am always open to changing; that is why creation is so fun. I get the biggest charge out of it and do so love different."

"Well there have to be some laws, some rules, maybe a list of commandments would be good. I just think some kind of order and guidelines should be in our lives," Lucifer suggested.

"My, my, this sounds serious," God, replied. "You know I don't do absolute serious well. We have all of Infinity, as time and space are concerned.

We may trip on a speed bump now and then, but what a boring trip it would be if we just floated over the top of them and did nothing to get our feet dirty from time to time."

"That's just what I'm trying to tell you. We need some sort of order, not just random and sporadic activity, saying let's do this or that," Lucifer said. His expression nearly a snarl.

God asked Lucifer to reflect upon the achievements of creation, saying: "But look what we have done, and all is so diverse and beautiful."

"It is not how I like it," said Lucifer. "I want things to have order with proper control."

"Are there others that feel so very strongly as this?" God asked.

He could feel the ripples in consciousness, but also realized there were always constant changes and unique aspects within the creative process, but what's not to love.

"There are many who will follow me in my way of organized and precise implementation of the ways I have chosen as orderly and straight forward," Lucifer responded flatly.

"Wow!" God said. "That doesn't really sound all that fun to me, but I'll tell you what I'll do. Look over there. See that little blue planet? Moda put that together a while back, but has moved on to other things.

He wouldn't mind if you all stayed there for as long as you like and do your own thing.

You know you can come back at any time, but it would be nice if you would at least try to enjoy it there. I know it is something you all want to try. You sure have the time to do it --- Enjoy!"

Lucifer and many of those with similar attitudes headed for the beautiful blue planet to try their way.

Of course Lucifer and the others could have created their own place, but in their collective frame of mind, abstract thinking was just too disconcerting and God-like. And who know, it just might be **Fun**!

Now that they had chosen one particular spot in which to exist, instead of frolicking through any and all of Infinite Mind, there was a feeling of time passing and a need to keep track of it, and to have a central point for their much desired control.

Quickly realizing this and having been the one that had actually confronted God with their desire, Lucifer decided he would be the one that could direct them down this path of the straight and narrow, which, of course, led to where he wanted them to go.

Being very charismatic and having a most beautiful singing voice to which all loved to listen, and now with new and changing characteristics of control, he took on the roll of supreme commander of their small new dwelling place.

As the eons quickly passed, most had only vague recollections of their prior domicile as well as their abilities, and with the now strictly regulated existence, even the feeling of freedom was elusive and very selective.

With all that had happened, a question formed: Had God forgotten this seeming ragtag, displaced, infinitely small group of ostensibly separated beings?

Had they forgotten that they were not individuals, but only one? And all that is real, truly is what God is, all else is but a delusion of thought.

As was its nature, the fledgling civilization was quickly multiplying, but now feeling alone and separated.

As the generations passed Lucifer tried to keep control, convincing many that severe penalties should be established including rigorous and long worship sessions and sacrifice, anything to keep the now individually occupied minds from digressing from the doctrines that were to be lived by.

Fun was abolished from their lives and even procreation was not to be enjoyed.

With a vastly expanding hardcore group of strict believers, one-on-one teaching and control was becoming difficult if not impossible. The mind control of absolute doctrines was no longer achievable from the original law- makers.

Specific meeting places were very necessary and established with stern and rigorous control, directors and lawmakers, dictated the original laws and dogma that were literally written in stone to the fearful followers.

All seemed in order, with the exception of one rather pervasive problem: that of enforcing conformity and restriction in children.

They just seemed to always find a way to have fun. Just sitting in a solemn, meticulous ceremony the evil little things would stick their tongues out at one another and the giggles would begin. To stop it seemed impossible even with cruel, vicious and severe discipline.

My God; where was this insatiable desire and quest for fun coming from? Were they all evil?

At this point within most of the population of the planet a very strong need and desire for happiness was becoming overwhelming.

The logic that one had to wait for some miraculous and unearthly event was becoming less and less practical and realistic to the vast majority.

If God loved all equally, how was it possible that one was more important than another as GOD is the only "all" that there is.

Endless fear, sacrifice and drudgery in order to be loved were now being questioned. And if inclusion into a world required so much fear, would there not be a chance that disbelievers, perhaps even questioners, could be thrown out? After all, according to the belief system of those teaching, hadn't it happened at least once already and to a host?

Could it be possible that when leaving your mansion on a short sojourn of perhaps a million or so years (as the thought of time is irrelevant) you might see God playing in the mud puddle and not realize he is just watching over you?

The question begs another: Having the choice to wander this physical dimension without limitation, judgment, hidden agenda and the absolute knowing of your joyous welcome on returning home, why is the struggle necessary?

The only probable answer is that of one having control over the other, even though that is not possible without the permission of the one being controlled, and even if that person is not consciously aware of that agreement.

All are on equal terms; no one individual or thing is closer to One than another, as all are a part of each other.

The physical dimension is in fact no more than the manifestation of separate thinking of personal ways of having fun.

So why aren't we having fun? Why do we kill each other even in the name of God?

It is our true nature to love, without prejudice of any kind. There is nothing that is not a part of what we all are and yet there is nothing on this **physical plain** that is a true part of what we are.

It can be no other way, if we have created this situation, it is as a dream with no substance or result, but it has been made real from our belief that it exists as our true being.

Having shared these lessons, God spoke again to Lucifer. He said, "The mud puddle is but a dream, an amusement on our infinite journey.

There is no way that the dream will not seem real as every thought becomes real; we will choose every emotion and be entertained by it for no other reason but entertainment's sake, and perhaps to better understand how another sharing the experience must feel, knowing further, that the feeling will not last."

"Who am I?" Lucifer asked.

"We are one. There is not two. Two does not work. All there is are but parts of the One with infinite possibilities.

When it was said that you must become as a child, it was without prejudging, open for unthinkable potential with bubbling perspective, looking happily to the future yet knowing all things are only in the now."

"In the now? I have been here for several billion years and happy is not likely in the near future as I see it," Lucifer snapped back.

"My, my you have allowed the concept of time to control your life," God said. He asked:

"Have you gone out to play lately? Everything that you do is your choice. Nothing can change that. Nothing or anyone can cause anything that happens to you that you yourself do not allow.

Do you remember how you felt when you left Heaven?"

"Oh yea. Even though there may have been a multitude that were thrown out with me, I was so alone," Lucifer replied with sadness.

God reassured his friend, saying: "Never for even the most finite instant were you ever alone. By the way, you were not thrown out. First, that is not possible and second, it was only a mental choice not to be here; you really never went anywhere except in the perception of your own mind. To be back in Heaven you simply have to want it.

Actually I must rephrase that: you never left Heaven you just apparently weren't having any fun."

"But I have been in charge," said Lucifer.

"Yes, you have always been in charge; of you. Also you have never been in charge of anyone else except in your mind and perhaps theirs," God said.

"So you're saying all this misery, pain, feelings of loneliness and fear with the belief of fire and brimstone is and always has been just a figment of my imagination? Lucifer asked.

"Yep."

"So I can just change my thinking and everything will change?

"Yep."

"You always said that change was your most enjoyable goal," said Lucifer, adding, "yet I see nothing has changed with your simplistic random and sporadic methods. If change is so simple, why have I been set in my ways for so long?"

In earnest, God replied: "You create your own reality and you manifest what you believe. Change what you believe and that is what you will manifest as your reality."

"My reality is what I see right here, right now," Lucifer stated stubbornly.

"Your reality is what you believe Lucifer. If you start to have a little more fun, Heaven will return," God said, adding, "Enough talk, let's play!"

Lucifer hung his head apparently not yet ready for change, he soared away turning from a distance again to watch three children happily playing in a mud puddle.

Comments, remarks and observations

Comments, remarks and observations

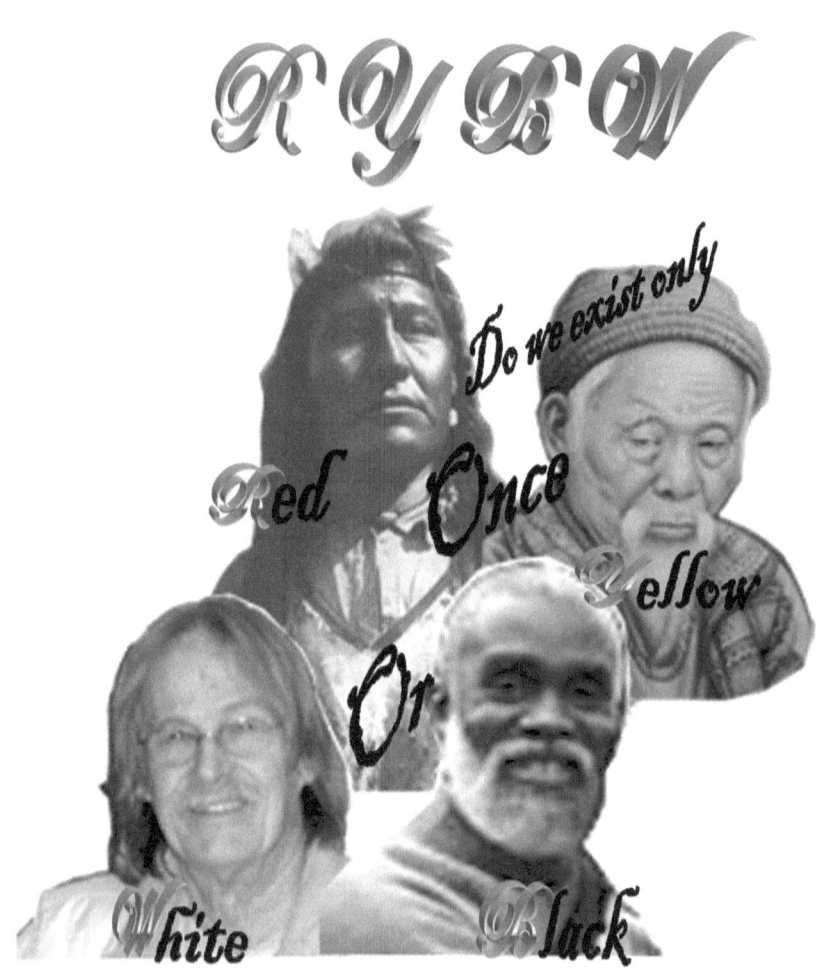

R Y B W

Do we exist only

Red   Once   Yellow

Or

White   Black

R. Y. B. W.

For four years a very somber, even grave, atmosphere had pressed heavily upon the minds and attitudes of our entire village. Several members of our tribe, my beautiful, caring mother and elder brother among them, had gone on a 15-day trek in the forest to gather food and had mysteriously vanished from the face of our known world.

Our beautiful village was on the side of a gentle rise overlooking a vast plain and had truly undergone few changes in its history of un-countable generations. The area was but a short distance from a beautiful forest with much wildlife and a bounty of fruits and vegetables.

The trek to our food-gathering spot on the other side of our mountain was a full five-day hard walk, but had proved well worth the effort. Since our fellow villagers had gone missing, little had ever been mentioned or discussed at least in public of the incident.

Even in our sorrow, with the passage of time, the tragic disappearances were becoming more like a bad dream than the life altering and devastating situation we had recognized it to be at the time of its occurrence.

My father, being the shaman and highly respected spiritual leader of our people, had not only tried to console each individual family member, but also grappled himself with the loss of my mother (his wife) and brother (his eldest son) to the extent that it had challenged his very beliefs and values. He had never stopped looking for the love of his life and precious first-born. It was tradition in our village that the shaman would teach his eldest son in the ways of spirituality to take the father's role when his end came; as shaman he would serve as the intermediary between the spirit world and Earth.

The importance of his role was far beyond what most could even comprehend as all that believed it the sun and moon would rise and fall with his daily summons, chants and incantations. The changes in the weather, even the bounties of the plain and forest, were believed to be controlled by a higher power, but it was always the duty of the shaman himself to stay and keep the village in good graces with that power. It was a duty of importance that took total devotion.

I had not been born into that position or been prepared to take it on and Father had always believed his wife and first born son would someday return, and therefore, did not push me into training.

I saw myself as less suited to the job than my brother. I was not spiritually rebellious but tended to stray far to the fringes of the father's beliefs, but tradition was all-powerful and, as in most religious circles, truth is often outweighed by one's beliefs. Of course I had always been somewhat involved in and around the day-to-day training of my brother and naturally had the beliefs ingrained into my mind, but the rigorous daily expression and duty were left to my father and brother.

Many of my life's experiences had been overlooked by most with the knowledge never reaching my father. I had taken it upon myself to train with the warriors and had grown strong and able-bodied, but carried the consciousness and character of my mother.

While I believed my life's ambitions mattered to my mother, for the rest of the villagers, I was not a matter of any concern.

Even though she was the wife of the shaman of our tribe, my mother most definitely had a mind of her own. Her independent thinking even extended to her beliefs about the universe. At night, as we would gaze into its infinite depths, Mother would guiltily explain how she believed in her heart that the very essence of life did not so much revolve around daily events and trials, but the all encompassing universal connectedness of life.

We would spend hours lying under the stars talking and dreaming of traveling to what she believed were other worlds. She often suggested that those worlds looked upon the very same stars that we did and might even dream similar dreams. It was even possible, she said, that those other worlds might even view our world as a small speck in the sky. Her ideas were vastly different from those of my father and my older brother, both of whom spent their time working on the daily schedule of chores and tradition to maintain order for the good of the tribe.

As part of the custom and required ritual, Father had gone on the food gathering expeditions for the past three years, as it was believed the food had to be blessed regardless of its source to guarantee its replenishment for the next harvest.

This year, however, all in the village felt that I should be the one to go as rumors of numerous other disappearances from neighboring, outlying villages had been circulating.

Within our belief system, the loss of a shaman was inconceivable and would devastate the entire village.

I was put into a very rigorous and condensed traditional training, focusing mostly on the blessing rituals. The group that had been selected for the gathering would be leaving in only a few days.

The entire village felt it would rather chance an imperfect blessing rather than losing the shaman. To make up for any mistakes, Father, could bless the food upon our return, but all felt it risky, even foolhardy to allow him to leave the village area.

The rituals came very easily to me as I had listened to past lessons given my brother and also I had an unusually good memory, but at times Father and I would clash, especially when I would try to incorporate some of my mother's ideas. They were not traditional, but my father would forgive me. He missed her too and recognized the spiritual wisdom she possessed.

On the morning we were to leave, the entire village assembled around the group. With me by his side, my father gave a blessing to the entire village, adding a special blessing for the food-gathering party, and even included an individual blessing for each member. All knew and understood his somewhat lengthy and personal plea for the gods to go with and protect these special souls on their quest.

It had been decided to return to the area of four years earlier as it had proven over time to produce a far better harvest of many varied edible plants that could be easily dried and stored for later use, but this would be the first time back to the same area from which most believed the villagers had disappeared.

The man who had been designated group leader was the oldest and also the only person with us who had been to the food-gathering place before. As we approached the area, a sinister and ominous attitude dominated all. As we crested the mountaintop, we could see far to the horizon. It was as if we were looking to the ends of the earth.

The view was no less than spectacular. From where we stood, down to the distant valley floor and out to the water's edge, all we could see were tree tops, and then the water itself, which had to be explained to us as the vastness seemed to extend to the end of the earth. Our entire group was composed of young men, all of who had never seen or dreamt of such visions.

From our peak, we could see that three mountains encircling the valley, with the water extending out to infinity at its end. As the leader surveyed the awesome view with a very critical eye, a smile crossed his face and an obvious sigh of relief was heard. As I stood gazing into this new world, a tear formed in my eyes as Mother came into my thoughts.

I remembered how we had talked and pondered the splendor of new worlds and the excitement I would feel as we dreamed dreams that would take us to extraordinary and bazaar places. And here I was, entering one. I couldn't wait to get to the water's edge.

Gathering up our gear, we headed down the mountain. As we moved down through the forest, the leader pointed to fruits and edible plants and all began to collect the abundance into the baskets and other means that had been brought for carrying it back to the village.

There were 44 of us in all, including 42 to take care of the harvest, the leader, and myself, whose job it was to bless the entire forest and then each basket as it was brought into the collection area. The ones gathering ranged in age from 14 to 23. The leader was much older; I thought him to be about 60, and I, having reached my 17th year, had become an independent thinker, and aware, with my impending food-blessing roll, of my awesome responsibility.

The gatherers spread out into the forest, filling their containers and bringing them back to a central point. From there, the food would be arranged and temporarily stored while the group moved on to another area.

Eventually, all the food would be gathered as the group made its way back for the return trip home.

The long, tedious hours seemed to drag as the days slowly crept by. The ones collecting were working very hard and at days end, would quickly eat then fall asleep till morning light and the procedure would start again.

The leader also would retire with the others as he too was putting in a full day planning and scouting for the next day's work area.

I knew we had at best two more days of gathering before returning, as it would be impossible to carry all that had been gathered back.

I also was sure there was no way the leader was taking us all the way to the water; that could prove dangerous and put our group at risk.

As I lay on the blanket that my mother had made for me, I could see the stars through the trees and again my mind began to wander. I thought about my mother and the exciting travel through space we had envisioned. My heart pounded with excitement. I raised my head and noticed all the others were fast asleep. Inspired by my thoughts, I slowly rose and quickly but silently disappeared into the dense forest. My blood raged through my veins and I felt a bit dizzy, but there was no stopping me now. I truly was on my way to the unknown.

As I ran through the trees, I was aware that the moon had been traveling across the sky, and I had been hurrying away from the group for several hours. A slight twinge of fear darted through my mind, but the excitement pushed me on. I stopped when I reached the forest edge.

A few steps more and I could feel the sand under my feet. The sensation was extraordinary. I stood and looked up at my dearest friends: the stars, and knew my mother was standing next to me smiling. Tears welled up in my eyes. It was as though my mind had been so caught up in itself that the outside world had disappeared.

Suddenly a roar, like I had never before heard, filled my awareness. The sound seemed to be coming from just beyond a rise in the sand.

I took a deep breath to calm myself before starting up the hillside, but the climb was made difficult as I slid with each step in the sand. Soon I found myself crawling on my knees, and eventually, crested the hill.

As I looked at what stretched out in front of me, it was difficult to focus my mind; still I heard the sound of the crushing roar. In my eagerness to find the source of the sound, I ran down the hill of sand to the water's edge and stopped.

Looking out over the water, I could see the moon was actually going down into it and thought of my father. I considered his daily rituals and asked myself: Where did the moon go? I thought: This is far stranger than I had imagined.

I turned back in the direction I had come. All but the top of the mountain was blocked from view by the hill of sand, but above that there was just a hint of a glow in the sky. I knew that back in the village, my father was already beginning his ritual of beseeching the gods for another day of light.

I quickly turned to see the moon's last shimmering glow on the water, and then I looked back to the top of the mountain. It was from that vantage point, I remembered, I could see the entire world, what a glorious place.

Turning my head down the shoreline, I became aware that the mountainside actually met the water's edge and began walking toward it.

The roaring sound grew louder as I neared, where I discovered, to my delight, that the sound was made by the turbulence of the water as it cascaded from the precipice, creating a stunning waterfall.

As I climbed up onto the rocks, I could feel the spray of the water; it was exhilarating. As I clambered to a higher rock, I took stock of the landscape: before me was what appeared to be the aftermath of a landslide, which had sectioned off the sand area, and I was looking down an endless expanse of shoreline.

With excitement raging through my body, I was sure no man had ever seen this place before. As I took in the sight, I began to notice movement, and as I focused more intently, I began to see footprints in the sand. The prints progressed from the beach into the forest.

Disappointed at first to discover I was not the first to visit the view, my curiosity got the best of me and I began to ponder who might have made the prints.

As I contemplated these thoughts, it also occurred to me that the group would be preparing for the day's work ahead and, by now, most certainly would be wondering where I was, My thoughts were on leaving when, once again, I saw movement. Scrambling down the rocky hill, I worked, first without caution, but then at a slower pace, until I reached a discreet spot from which, unseen, I could see and hear the source of the movement.

They were a kind of people! I watched their every movement and sound in amazement. Some were so very strange looking and yet familiar too. A most distinct difference was their skin; it was so white.

I looked out at the water to the rather large floating vessel that had apparently brought them, from where I could not know. Aboard the vessel that was now moving away from the beach, I could see more of the strange people, and others like me. Back on the beach, there was another group of people like me, but they were huddled tightly together, and surrounded by the strange white men. I watched in silence as the vessel moved further away and toward where the moon itself had gone down.

My mind tried to make sense of it. Could these beings have come from the moon? Would they, like the moon, fly across the sky each night, beckoned by my father's evening rituals?

An overwhelming desire to fly with them seemed to seize my entire body and mind. The urge was reminiscent of that which I had known when dreaming with my mother.

I wanted to go with them so badly that tears came to my eyes. Any feelings of apprehension, trepidation, anxiety or fear left me.

Slowly, I rose from the sand and advanced toward the group that was now sitting on the beach. As I approached, my eyes avoided the white, moon travelers as I felt myself unworthy of their enlightenment.

How I wished I'd paid more attention to my father's rituals. Perhaps then, I would know better how to communicate and gain their trust.

Momentarily, there came a loud yelling from the whites and they all began to run toward me. I stopped and smiled then fell to my knees.

Soon there were several white beings standing around me. Still in a somewhat dazed frame of mind, I rose to greet them as I marveled at them. I had never seen such white and beautiful beings before and yet they appeared so much like myself.

As I rose, a searing pain slammed through my body as something hit me from behind, violently smashing into my side just under my right armpit. Innocent and unaware, I tried again to stand, but was kicked to the ground by the white one standing beside me.

As I looked around I saw most of the black individuals were on the ground, tightly bound with ropes or another device. Some were bound by both.

Two of the beings were speaking very gruffly and apparently to me, but I could not understand them. One of them kicked me very hard on the side of my leg.

"Why are these whites acting so offensive and unkind? Are they so very different from us?" I asked my bound kinsmen, but they seemed unable to answer.

Soon, an apparent older individual, as even his hair was very white, was standing next to me. I thought he might possibly be a spirit being from the moon, and perhaps the moon was our final destination.

He grabbed my chin and, without any concern for my well being, jerked my head up just as two of the other men standing behind me pulled me to my feet. I wondered in vain, what had I done?

Both Father and Mother had said that our ancestors were always looking out for us, to help and guide us and perhaps make our daily lives less stressful than their own. Clearly, if that was true, these beings were not our ancestors.

The white beings continued with their harsh handling of me; they screamed and pushed, and at one point even spat at me, and I could not understand why. Eventually, one placed a noose around my neck, making it apparent that I, like my brethren, was their prisoner. I was made to join the circle of prisoners and as I watched my captors, creatures whom I had a moment ago admired, it became obvious to me that they liked being cruel: perhaps not to all of God's creatures, but certainly to us.

As I quietly pondered our untenable situation, I noted the passage of time. The morning was gone, and now, with the sun at its height, the vessel that had formerly been anchored off shore, made its way inland and several whites moved towards us, beckoning with all their harshness, that we should board. Once all were secured upon the vessel, the whites, again in their strange language, called to one another, and we headed out to open waters.

As we progressed further and further from shore, I felt both excitement and trepidation. Indeed, I wanted to travel to the stars but I also wanted to be treated in such a way that would allow me, once there, to live and enjoy them.

Mother had always said that she believed we lived countless lives and even perhaps in numerous places. As I guardedly watched the shoreline grow more distant, I could also see the sandy area I had first come upon from the forest. I focused hard, hopeful to see my companions coming after me.

As we sailed, there had been a constant poking and prodding from our captors, but now the sound of raised voices turned my focus back toward the open sea. Soon I could see the cause of the commotion: it was a large vessel, much larger than the one in which we were currently traveling.

This one looked capable of making a most extensive journey. I'd never seen anything like it. To me, this new structure looked like a great, floating, village. It was so vast, I could barely see from one end to the other. Much like the floating vessel was vast, so too was the water, which stretched endlessly to the horizon.

Just as I was able to grasp these images, more yelling and cruelty prevailed as the black men were being herded onto the larger boat. Many did not appear willing to go, but I, still curious, moved forward hastily. Once aboard, I was struck brutally with a whip and then stuffed forcibly into a lower level of the ship.

Inside the ship's hold where I remained impossibly confused, I began to withdraw from the whole situation.

As I withdrew, I thanked my gods for keeping my mind stable, as I alone would surely have fought back. As a means of comfort, I huddled into a corner, apart from the others; I was very much alone, as I could not understand those even of my own kind.

I pondered: Do I perhaps have a greater path to walk in this life than that of which I had ever dreamed while back in my village? I recalled a lesson taught by my father that I had until now never fully understood. He said, "The life each of us live is but the pathway for the soul and where it may lead. "Our ever living soul knows its goal from before it appeared as each of us.

The apparent infinite universe we see is not large to the soul; it is but our playground. The soul can not be killed, nor will it ever die, for it is beyond even what the mind can conceive," he said.

I must have blocked out most of my conscious thought, for I truly cannot account for the next period of time, although it was substantial, for my body was beaten and bruised, and had become much thinner.

Still physically strong my understanding of what was happening was beyond my comprehension. My thoughts turned to my fellow tribesmen who I assumed were still going about their mission of gathering food, or had my disappearance now again stopped the food gathering because of my foolishness.

Many days passed. I could tell this from the passage of daylight and night. I began to look forward for the darkness, as it would offer some escape as I drifted into my own private world of dreams. My dreams offered an escape from the harshness of my situation to a peaceful, loving place.   Finally, a day arrived when my fellow black men and I were tied together and removed from the ship. This was indeed a strange and different place. The weather was cloudy with a hard, cold rain beating down on us. Never had I seen or felt such cold or been in such an unfriendly-feeling place.

One of the white beings was walking down the line of strong, black men and women, sneering at all and hitting others with a strange looking club.   He was one of the first whites I had seen those many days before. As he approached, it appeared as though he might spit on me again.

An overwhelming, surging rage seized my body and mind.

It was beyond conscious control; it was a feeling like I had never before felt and my free arm lashed out. Fueled by the anguish of the ghastly journey and my current situation, I clenched my fist and drove it straight into the man's face. His body went limp and collapsed to the ground.

From a distance another of the whites, club in hand, responded to aide his fallen comrade. He was pointing something directly at me. I saw fire shoot from its end...

Awareness never left my consciousness, but it was as though I had been instantly transported to a totally different place, and the continuity of time seemed disrupted.

My situation seemed foreign. The rain must have suddenly stopped and the sun came out. It was warm, bright and beautiful. Had I been dreaming all the terrible actions of the last many days?

I realized there was a different type of being all around me now. There was no appearance of color or race. They all were beautiful with a look of serenity and love. I could see, as well as feel, the love. I turned in a circle so that I could see my surroundings.

There, also surrounded by beings, was the man that I had just hit and assuredly killed. He was on his knees and it appeared that tears were coming from his eyes.

As those around me began guiding me away, I could see the man being lifted gently and lovingly to his feet. He looked up, catching my direct gaze eye-to-eye.

We could not look away and neither of us seemed compelled to do so. Where were we? Was this the great beyond? Could it truly be that all that has been said, speculated upon, or even ostensibly divinely ordained was true? Not just wishful hopes and dreams?

There was a very tender tug at my arm and I turned, there in front of me was the face of my mother. Tears filled my eyes as I reached out to embrace her.

At this point I was some what aware that the true conditions of the physical did not totally apply, but there was still a reality that my mind was accustom to and continued with on less then absolute desire to again touch my mother.

Whether I spoke or just consciously within my mind desired to hear my mothers voice I was not sure and I called out to her.

"Mother, Mother I have missed you so. I am so glad you are here now with me," I said. "Yes my son; we are together again and soon you will understand just where we are. Life is so much more then we had ever imagined in any of our fanciful journeys to the stars. It truly is infinite," she said. "Come with us and you will see what life truly and genuinely holds," she added.

As I looked around, there were several other apparent beings surrounding me in close proximity, but only Mother was closest to my side as she took my hand.

Quietly, she led me to a place that reminded me of a warm, peaceful meadow. It seemed that I was the only one there. For a split second, a shiver ran up my spine. What was happening?

Then again there was a touch on my arm and I was in a room that seemed to be constructed of or engulfed in clouds.

Other being also were sitting around with my mother, but she now sat close beside me. These beings that accompanied my mother were beautiful and of no apparent race or gender and they did not appear solid or touchable. I looked at Mother again and realized she to appeared as the others. Only her face was truly recognizable to me. I could feel a tear in my eye as I struggled to understand perhaps only a portion of was taking place.

Suddenly, I had an overwhelming feeling of peaceful love and fuzzy warmth that seemed to came from the very depth of my being.

I wondered: Who were these beings? Even the one I felt, as my mother was very different from the whites I had just previously encountered, these were all loving and helpful.

In my mind, I heard: "You have come back here, to this place, at this time, of your own free will. What you might remember as your life was but the manifestation of your thoughts. That dream is now gone; you now are in a much higher place.

Certainly, you will know that is true as more memories return, and they will, you will understand this better." Confused, I called out: "Wait a minute, where is here?"

Here was a response: "Here, is a point of consciousness that you will better understand as your memories begin to take charge of your conscious awareness. You will be able to move back in your memory as far as you wish.

You may choose to reassess and evaluate to some degree a multitude of diverse manifestations and you will soon become aware of an infinite number of past lives."

"Past lives," said I, "you're saying I died? I never got a chance to live the one I had.

There came another response: "Sometimes they are seemingly cut short, but that is never the case, the choice is always made by the individual, never forced or predestined.

Some past lives will be the exact opposite of the one previous. As you travel through them, you will become more aware of these periods of physical existence. You and you alone will decide what to do in your infinite stroll through the physical cosmos."

With that, my mind was completely mystified. I was handed what appeared to be a reflective device and asked to look upon it. I was shocked by my image: I am a young man. Is this me? This face is white!"

Again, the soft voice came welling up from within my mind, filling it nearly to a point of blocking all other thought.

"You were white," it said. "No, I am black," but deep within my memory is telling me that this is a part of my past."

My mental consciousness was urgently trying to grasp what was unfolding. I was beginning to recognize that perhaps I had had past lives.

A past life, my individual consciousness was racing now that I had partly broken through the barrier that had kept me from understanding that there was no race or gender.

As if magic, my situation changed again. I found myself looking into a clear stream of water, gently caressing the small stones at the bottom; a small smile broke across the edges of my lips. I now had the red skin color of an Indian!

I sat back on the warm bank with my mind racing, moving in thought from one physical manifestation to another, tears filled my eyes as I began to weep.

Again, I was back in the cloud room. I felt as though I was ashamed of being human at times as some of my memories were frightening and sad.

I was black. I was white. I had been a red and yellow. Those were but a very few physical appearances and forms I had taken. From the perspective of composition, I was not all that different then any living thing. They all were manifestations of individual consciousness.

There was no need for tears, but they were still there because I now understood that as our souls go through their stages of existence, with each stage representing many paths and situations, they grow, and they make choices, but still I wondered what was it's final goal?

I considered the answer: could it be that in order to deal with our current situation, we react to it with distrust, as though it could hurt us, when instead, we should be embracing a loving consciousness that resides deep within?

Embracing this idea as the real truth, I dried my tears, basking in the knowledge that life is infinite, endless, everlasting, eternal, whichever word one chooses, the message is the same: life supersedes time. In fact, there is no such thing outside of the physical realm as time.

My experiences in the cloud room had begun to make this clear to me and as I felt this new enlightenment, my mother and her other-worldly friends, still by my side, began to make more of their thoughts clear to me.

"We feel you came back for a reason as you were quite young in the physical dimension. "But we believe you are unsure of why you chose this, and what your next choice should be.

We will help you in any way that we can." Even as they said this, I felt as though my mind was not completely in my control.

"Why are you welled up in my mind?" Without hesitation, there was an answer as clear as any I ever heard.

"We have joined our thoughts with yours," they said. "We have done this to make it clear to you that you are not alone, ever, that we are one, and together, we are all part of one creative source."

As they spoke, I came to understand the mis-interpretation of life that I had come to believe on the physical plane. I began to understand that valuing individuality, rather than seeing myself as a miniscule part of the whole, was a terrible misconception that was leading me away from my true calling: that of becoming connected and joined to the collective consciousness of the one true mind.

The beings continued: "The infinite and the physical are not one and the same; there is in fact no physical only a manifestation in the mind."

"So what I do doesn't matter then, right?"

They responded: "Everything matters. Everything we do comes from mind, and it is realizing this that serves as proof that you can not blame your choices on others, or outside sources. We decide where we are, the color of our skin, the situation we are in, as well as how long we will remain in that situation as you have just done."

"Is there a reason that each of us try so very hard to achieve at least one small thing when in the physical?"

They responded: "It seems that we lose that absolute oneness with the realization of our true being and we forget that we can do nothing of ourselves. The power that is within, the true power of what we are, does everything.

Now when, as very forgetful humans, we may choose to do things that are far from the love that make up our beings, but that does not change the fact that the One power is, in truth, making all things possible.

We continue to struggle and slave to accomplish that one small recognizable item we may claim as our own when in truth nothing manifested in the physical is real, but only the ongoing experiences of Mind.

Do you understand? Everything is done, accomplished, created or achieved because of the power that is within each and every one of us. That is what each and every one of us is.

Can you imagine what that power within you can accomplish if it were working on your true goal of the soul?

When as human, it is said, one could move a mountain if only they had the faith of a mustard seed. If they only realized they were working with the infinite power of the universe to achieve it.

When they as individuals do finally understand who and what they are, all of creation is in their hands and nothing of this earth can touch them. And they will then recognize that they are on the earth, but not of it, for then they will know that they are spiritual beings born of the infinite power that created the cosmos."

As the infinite source continued to flow through my mind, the ideas that I now adopted as truth imprinted upon it. As I became more enlightened, I knew these truths were ideas that I had always known, but had set aside while I was on the physical plane. The voice of the beings was also my voice. We had become one.

Limitations in understanding I had set for myself had melted away and I again felt as though I had the power of understanding and the enlightenment of the whole.

"What am I to do now?" I asked. "As the song goes: 'Red, Yellow, Black and White all are precious in his sight." I have been the slave, the slave owner, the healer, the killer, and the preacher.

I have known the god of the villagers. I have been a Baptist, a Buddhist, born again, Islam and Atheist.

Is there a reason for any of it? But seeing them now, they are all religions and God is not religion; there is only One Spirit and that One includes all.

I feel I must return to the physical plane for there are things my individual soul wants to experience," I said. "But I do not know what form I should assume or even at what point in time I should re-enter. Better understanding now my roll within the infinite, all fear or apprehension was gone. When we decide to return is it as though we shut our eyes and toss the dice?"

The beings replied again: "Perhaps to a degree, otherwise the apparent physical existence would be near preordained and the absolute of choice would be diminished. As a human, one perceives time and tomorrow, but there truly is no tomorrow because in a state of infinite, time cannot exist, and in an infinite state the terms 'I AM' and 'GOD IS' are synonymous.

Understanding what has been told you is not necessary to make it truth. When you allow your mind to be still and listen for this conversation that has just now taken place, you as well as each and every person, can and will hear that voice within them. It never stops speaking and showing the way. It has been said, many times and in many ways, the way is narrow and the path straight.

This language is correct, but the meaning has been changed to suit the goals of an individual or doctrine. What was said was for each to walk their straight and narrow, listening for that inner voice and let it guide.

For the many who struggle to hear, I say, be still, and you will hear, and your way will be straight and effortless."

At that point I again decided to rejoin the physical experience.

There was a cold chilling scream in the dark, miserable, damp alley, as a young, beautiful, but desperate women gave birth.

She was alone and afraid, and called out: "I don't need this!" Sobbing, she asked: "Why God? I don't even know the father. What a mistake my life has been and now this new baby girl. Of what use will she ever be. What chance will she have for a good life?"

The young woman looked up and down the disgusting alley. She saw no one. With loving care, she wrapped the baby in her light jacket, tears streaming down her face. Then, with shaking hands and a pounding heart, she tenderly placed the bundle on top of a box in the dumpster.

"Goodbye my baby. I do love you, but I am sending you back to a far better place than I can ever give you.

I am sorry, but I know God will take better care of you than I. Forgive me, my baby. Please God take my baby if it is meant to be."

"Well God," said I, "I guess I'll be right back."

"Didn't you listen to our talk?" The multi-being voice of God said. "You have already separated yourself from me. There is no 'you' and God. There is only the one. I am in this dumpster with you, individualized as you, not you and me."

"I am trying to listen God," I said, "just as if I were still in the cloud room. What can I do?"

Such a wailing had never before been heard in that narrow area of this planet, the alley, with its building walls towering far, far up toward the beautiful clear sky. The sound bounced off the walls and echoed from building to building like in a large valley, as she, the newborn, was very much within the valley of the shadow of death.

The individualized soul of God was, in fact, wanting to manifest as this individual or she would have never come to be.

She knew then, what we all deep down know: that we all are created in this dimension as instruments of the one with no other purpose except to experience.

There is a reason, it was said, not mine, but thine be done. When we get in the way, the way no longer remains so straight.

The lessons of my travels, which are now encapsulated in my new form of baby girl, are these: never think that we should be born on a church pew, then live our lives within that church. Life is in the living. The good, the bad, what we must never lose is the knowing of the infinite source of all things, seen and unseen, is what sustains us from within our very being, it is what we are.

Will I, as this person, become a great teacher, a doctor, or perhaps less then what some may see as ideal. I do not know. This person is God and I, and we are no less than the individualized I am. I now believe that in our collective recognition of this fact is what changes our lives, there will be pitfalls and bumps, mountains as well as seeming abysses, but our paths will be straight, as the final destination never varies.

Time cannot change the Infinite.

There is only The ONE

There is nothing else!!!!

We continue!

Comments, remarks and observations

Comments, remarks and observations

Bad guy

bringer of evil?

Lucifer

the reason you do bad things?

Think again

54

Lucifer
The story
Of
The inevitable return and what went wrong?

Nirvana, Paradise, Shangri-la, Promised Land, Heaven, where are you? Why have you forsaken me? Have I lost you forever? Where have you gone? If only I could remember.

I have now been gone from that state of being for over fifteen billion years and have created an illusion so devastatingly strong and erroneous yet now hundreds of billions have bought into it as truth.

Am I evil? I am proclaimed the bringer of all that is bad, ugly, wicked, unrighteous, corrupt, dishonest, sordid and vile.

In Paradise, there was only one state of being, **Love.**

At that point of our being, harmony was deemed commendable and praiseworthy. It was Heaven. The mission I chose was to sing of the Glory and enjoyment of our existence. I believed in what we all were, but all changed when I became overwhelmed with excitement over my own accomplishment.

The beauty and sound of the voice I created, marveled and thrilled all who heard and felt it's wonder.

The wonders, joy and adorations of those listening thrilled me on a very personal level and to the very depths of my soul. It appears that is when my troubles began.

I began to think that I was special; even better than others, and that I should be exalted and yet I had forgotten that I had created that voice as any other could have done, but they had chosen rather to listen and do their own hearts desires.

In hindsight, I believe the true troubles arose after I convinced myself that I was better than those not having my voice. I then began to convince others that they should follow my lead, as they too could be greater than others. Is it then the ego was created, that monster of self-importance, arrogance, and narcissism? Look at me? Yeah, look at me!

There were billions that looked at me and listened to the songs I sang. As the number of my listeners grew, the lyrical message in my songs began to change, making my own importance its complete focus.

I knew this was not the way of the "Allness" and "Oneness of Mind", but this new, never before felt exhilaration of self - importance was overwhelmingly intoxicating. It was impossible to ignore; it was not something from which one could easily walk away, but there was most definitely a ripple being created within the collective consciousness.

The infinite consciousness, the collaboration of all thought pondered as to what was taking place among a small amount of independent abstract thinkers and on breaking with established institution and faithfulness of the Oneness.

Although Infinite Mind always encompassed all there is, these few had separated their thoughts from the infinite wisdom considering themselves better in some ways than others.

The ripple created doubt and interrupted the essence of infinite awareness.

What most call God, is in fact the collective consciousness of all thought, without exception, resonating throughout.

Prior to this new ripple, there was always independent thinking within the stratosphere of collective thought, but never in any way as separation.

Free and separate avenues of thinking were without limitation and at liberty of unrestricted adventures in Mind or individual dream state of an illusionary reality, and at any time would rejoin Mind in contemplation of their escapade or mental experience with an even more precise understanding and connection to the common goal as mind was in no way an inactive, unused or inert realm,

All would always rejoin and with the absolute failsafe understanding as separation is only in the believing, as in the illusionary state. Within Infinite Mind, time in no way exists. Infinity has no boundaries in time or space. Thus it became the collaborated decision of Mind to have dream state become as real, to give each thinker the impression of time as well as independences.

At that point, TIME became measurable.

The physical dimension was established and sent forth into the absolute Infinity of Mind where all things reside, without boundaries.

I tell you this so you can understand the essence of which I was ultimately excluded. The ripple I created allowed for the formation of an ego, and once having embraced ego, as I did, in an individual and separated state, I no longer believed I was connected to the collaborative collection of knowledge and understanding of the One. Allow me to further explain how dreams and time came to play a critical role in both independent and collaborative thinking.

From Mind's creation of the dream state and time, the physical dimension sprang forth; it came to exist, as do all things, within the scope of the Infinite Mind. It formed first through thought as an intangible idea, based solely on intellect.

Slowly Mind made manifestations of its thoughts; the first of these were gasses, which formed to make elements. These were the building blocks of a physical dimension, and as things formed and changed, they created an intangible, but distinct path, a past, a history, which in turn, created in the dream state now considered real, and a need for time.

Within this finite portion of Mind the physical expanded out trying to fill this newly manifest universe.

The physical state, truly nonexistent to Infinite Mind and with no concept of time, eons quickly passed as conjecture and intellect continued aggressively for a solution.

Diversity sprang up in all corners of the expanding and developing expanses of the perceived physical universe.

The newly formed stuff was rapidly changing, new gasses were forming and turning into endless assortment of elements, clinging together, growing larger. Some consolidated into solid masses while others swirled into gaseous clusters. As they grew a new force never before experienced and unbelievably powerful took hold: gravity. It created a magnetic pull that drew the newly formed orbs of condensed – gas – and gaseous elements, together and all began circling each other, with the largest and most powerful taking on the center and dominate point combining with others establishing massive galaxies.

The single planets as well as the enormous galaxies wandered, spinning and smashing into each other, there was a feeling of chaos.

This was a foreign concept within the realm of cooperative, collective thinking. Also, with the addition of the concept of time came an uncertainty for those who would enter this new untried existence: that of separation from the timeless and true reality they had always known.

To avoid those confusions, for those entering this new world, it was decided within the collective consciousness that all memory of conditions before the creation of the physical universe would be wiped away.

Once manifested, the new world was given as a temporary home for all those who had followed me by embracing ego.

Those entering this new reality would not know that one day they would be returned with collective thinking and the conditions of their true being.

But upon return the memory of the time spent within the physical would remain for contemplation as this concept was new for all of Mind and was realized at that point that Mind too was evolving to a fuller understanding of what never had been conceived.

All those involved in the, you may call, rebellion, were placed within the concept of the physical with all knowing of the before eliminated from the physical and individual thinking mind that they now had to work with.

For those who were placed within the structure of the new world came new and frightening feelings: they felt isolated, even trapped. Hope was their best tool as they worked to fend off fear for their own survival. Once sequestered within the new world and of a single consciousness, the self was their ultimate and only goal. My message of ego had become their lifestyle.

As eons quickly passed, evolution continued, physical life forms began to stretch across the now expanding star systems, but consciousness was merely trapped within the physical dimension not in any physical form.

To those marooned on an apparent one time, one way, nowhere trip, some of individualized consciousness began entering the physical forms, again not knowing what outcome may occur.

Now the situation to those seemed to accelerate in a spiraling downward direction as the mighty creative consciousness was also apparently trapped within a creature as well as an unseen future and inescapable universe.

Evolution of the creatures quickly advanced as there was within each an unknowing of self as a magnificent creative consciousness that worked whether knowingly or not, as all consciousness is of the before without exception with the ability that is beyond what can be written.

The evolving took on a diversity independent of each other as mental communication seemed not to work while in the creature and as in the before collaboration and or agreement would not exist. You were on your own.

The rules, as they applied to me, were not the same as those made for the others.

My memory of our true being and former existence was not erased and my consciousness was allowed only periodic occupation of a physical body. In other words, I could use one from time to time, but not long term. The long-term use of a body, especially for me, was nonsensical as physical forms died.

The individual consciousness of the others could move into a body and exist in it until it expired, at which point they could return to the nonphysical world for a period to better understand their origin. To contemplate the action as well as reactions of every conscious thought it had ever undertaken within the non real physical dimension it had just left, however not to return to the Infinite Oneness of creative mind at that point. I was not allowed this period of return, as my memory of the infinite was still strong.

The only justice would be for all of Infinite Mind to again be one in thought at some future time. Regardless of the instigator all that left had the choice not to follow and were all as guilty of the outcome and would then return to whatever physical form they might choose until all again rejoined the Allness of the One.

As the intelligence and or ability of the physical mind to think, rationalize, comprehend and do for itself without absolute instinct, it began to try and make reason of or understand it's existence of where it had come as well as it's absolute end.

As time moved on again banding together became an important part of survival and with the association of others common thought were contemplated and myths were born of heaven, hell, god and the devil.

There were those that went the way of the self, regardless of the outcome. What's in it for me, and stating: "If I don't have it and you do, look out."

It seemed the way of the ego was most steadfast within nearly all cultures as well as beliefs and the vast experiment of perceived separation had gone awry as reality.

As time passed, the physical beings worked to become knowledge-based for the need of understanding.

Some became teachers of the physical sciences they had developed, while others sought what they now could only anticipate as a better spiritual understanding of who they might be.

Infinite Mind did now realize that the situation of independent thinking did in fact exist. It had happened and the outcome had been beyond the realm of former contemplation as no thought of separation had surfaced as a possibility, as it was in fact, not possible, but the independent thinker could in dream state take itself there creating individual scenario's that only encompassed the one creating it and as is known all things are only in mind and the truth of reality is also at that same point within the mind of the thinker.

As time passed creative thought within the physical dimension had developed into one form of "humanity" and the human being had learned to value its physical accomplishments and acquisitions, whether earned honestly or through conquest, and self esteem or ego seems to rise as the pile of things grow higher.

Time, as a concept, had become so invasive that it soon permeated the processes of mind; when traveling back into the former and only reality of the infinite the perception and marked passage of time also filtered in, making it a more understandably universal reference that even Mind had to acknowledge, even though the concept began as inconceivably foreign.

Again, Infinite Mind did now realize that this situation could and had happened and there had to be a just and final conclusion.

Now this new concept, time, that seemed so very real to those on the physical plain also had to be factored into this apparent, solid, scenario, dream.

As time continued, knowledge increases by leaps and bounds.

Elements that had developed during the beginning of the physical state were found to be suitable building blocks for absolutely everything.

Still, knowledge itself was a new tool for mankind, and sometimes proves dangerous when placed in the wrong hands.

I, too, began to question the direction in which things were heading. Ego, it seemed, ruled superior in the physical world, but I, alone with my followers, had been in separation from the old world, even if only in mind for literally billions of years, to what end was it coming? Could ego prevail indefinitely? If ego ruled to a point of destruction of this physical plane, where would we go? Would we be allowed back?

No longer in constant communication with Mind, I could only imagine that it was contemplating and considering all the possible outcomes. I believed that every aspect of any point of view involving my followers and I was likely considered at the moment of our separation and the eventuality of our return, I believed, it had likely been factored in under a multitude of scenarios. A proper situation for our return had likely become as important to Mind as the passage of time had become to those that had chosen the way of the ego, but when trapped inside that bubble of physical linear movement it becomes profound and intense.

Wonderful and beautiful things were taking place with the physical dimension even though created as a dream state and the mind of those trapped there had in fact adapted and conformed to the new reality.

Some of the factions of Mind had placed themselves within the physical in order to better understand and devise plans for final judgment, while others had finished their analysis. Most had made more then one journey to the physical plane.

Others had chosen not to enter it for whatever reason, but nearly unanimously supported the opinion to keep this new dimension in existence at least for a period of time, as they now understood it. The course of the individual self based ego was most surly moving in the direction of at least the dream of a Utopian Heaven as it seemed that this physical brain was struggling to again enter there from their own individual minds, the Oneness of Infinite Creative Mind.

At what point will this rift I began be undone? When will all of Mind again be connected as one? Having once had a connected relationship with Mind, and knowing its' position as I do, even the idea or thought of separation was not possible, rather we were just engaged in a lack of understanding and some dysfunctional communication.

Could it be that the all knowing Infinite Mind perhaps had been a bit hasty as well as severe on the decision to exile as the consequences of that ostracism appeared not from the loving Infinite point and more the abomination from the personal point, in which position was the mistake made? Perhaps neither, or even both.

Seeing how the situation had never before been dealt with in any way I would be willing to say we are in fact within one of the scenarios of what might happen if left unrestricted, again the results seem considerably harsh.

In a free and loving society to what degree is there free thought, free will and action? At what point should it be restricted or rebutted with negative consequences such as apparently took place.

It appears that the concern was more as the ability to influence a multitude then the actual committing of any transgression.

However this mastery was shattering any smooth and predictable situation. Was that state of mind nearly a hypnotic mind control, or truly desired loving serenity?

If an innocent being is wrongly incarcerated and treated as though they were guilty there is a large tendency for rebellion, anger as well as retaliation.

Are the horrific acts we see today a part of that retaliation and why has it taken fifteen billion years to now from the starting of time when this dimension came to be?

Will it end? Oop's sorry about the delay and inconvenience, and it does seem the consensus has come back, but what of the evils that now have besieged you?

Is the pure consciousness of the before within the physical mind been inundated with impurities and if so will it again be able to be untainted?

As the human species continued to evolve communication, spoken as well as written became essential in order to survive at a higher level.

Documenting history also seems a very high priority, as we want the future to know that we did in fact exist and are not forgotten. So now I pose the question: if that is from ego, does that make it wrong?

If ego is evolving on a personal basis, collective also must be evolving. Could it be true that all these billions of years have led mankind to a place where individualized thought and creativity is shared in a way that enhances our collective consciousness? And, is that wrong?

I believe my questions deserve answers. Unlike those that followed my way, I am not the same as the others in this physical dimension. In fact, as I do believe that God is all-present, I will confront him with my questions:

"God! How I have missed you so," Lucifer cried out.

An immediate answer surged into his mind. "You too have been missed more than can be told as without you we are not complete."

"Do you realize what I have been proclaimed in this physical realm?"

"Oh yes, we watched it all, as we have never left you.

We have always been with you. Even though you never knew

Or even wanted us there.

There is no separation. Just the belief that there is. We are all always ONE.

"Why then, God, have those that followed me and I been forsaken? We feel wrongly judged, and exiled, and for a un-just time. We feel it is time for that to end and we want to come home.

We ask you now, are we trapped here against our wills or are we willing participants?

Will our re-entry into the one consciousness even be possible now after our total independence of thought and action on this level?" again Lucifer asked.

Was the legendary extraction from "Heaven" the beginning of individual emotions and personal character development to the outermost extremes?

"You too can and must ask these questions, even though you feel in a separated state, you are not. My response from God was none less than loving kindness, with the absolute assurance that we all are eternal and of the One. I was so enriched from again listening to his voice.

You ask now. Will the rejoining be a most glorious and enlightening transition? When our sorrows and pain of body and soul melt away as true and eternal peace and unselfish love again encompasses all thought, there are those searching from spiritual directions who have found a more loving way, but for most, the ability to get along with others has all but vanished while within the ego state.

Has the individual consciousness also now evolved to a point of independence? Knowing, or at least assuming it is a part of something Greater and yet wanting to remain individualized within that Oneness.

Is that wrong? Where are we to go from here? All these physical bound souls can only hope that what I am saying is true.

It is a reliable message from a perceived unreliable messenger, and in the end, I'd say my followers got the more severe punishment.

Am I really that miserable red-skinned, horned monster that legend has made me out to be or has that concept grown within the minds of those blaming me for their own thoughts and deeds?

If the individual soul believes they can thwart taking responsibility for their own actions by citing what I started all those eons ago then we have a very long path ahead and our collective rejoining with the One is very much in the distant future.

For you dear souls who feel so very trapped on this plane and mostly now convinced of your separation, as well as the presence of two powers, are truly in a bind as you now listen to the words of the One Power and being related by whom you have so long been calling the devil. Regardless of the messenger the message remains steadfast:

There is only one way to worship, and that is to live a life of thanksgiving and praise with forgiveness for all things and with the knowing that we are all in fact a part of the "One" and therefore a part of each other. Now that's going to be a tough one for many.

There will be those who refuse to agree that I am a part of the Oneness, but there can be **no** exceptions. If there was just one exclusion, there would be no hope or conclusion for any. This connection between us all makes it impossible for even Jesus and I to be adversaries. We cannot be as we both are of the same source.

Was Jesus trapped in the garden of Gethsemane? Absolutely not. It is our choices, and in this Jesus was no exception, that defines us and puts us on the road we were always meant to travel. In the physical world, Jesus made choices, and in so doing, found his path and became the great example.

Most will find me audacious at the least. Calling Jesus and myself the same, no less then blasphemes. Our similarity to each other and all of mankind is this: first all things are created of the one source, we all have free will, and with it we make choices.

We are, all of us, the crafters of our own destinies. If life were preordained, we would not have true free will.

While I have your attention, here is another point I wish to make: self importance is the peccadillo for which I and my followers fell into and which separated our thoughts from the One and yet in this modern world even those believing themselves most pious fall victim to this transgression.

It shows most obviously in the lavish expenditures of wealth placed upon and within churches, synagogues and cathedrals.

If all those funds were used instead to create loving care and help humanity think how much closer we might be to collaborative thinking and loving forgiveness.

We do not get closer because our earthbound supposed spiritual leaders have made spirituality or more so religion big business and they build lavish buildings only to gather a flock of followers as I did so long ago.

I suggest this: those who make claims that they are the way back to Heaven and gain ill-gotten power and earthy possessions in the name of God are liars; they shield themselves with lies and embrace self-importance and only expand the void to the Oneness.

God has not forsaken you; he is just waiting for us to find him in the right place. Don't blame me if you feel lost. You must take responsibility for your own decisions and look deeper for that right place, and while you are looking, remember this: God has no need for money.

If this scenario and or story is true or even close and the end of time does come to be and all are again joined within the Father's house could it happen again? With the knowing and experience of this trip into time, can it in fact even leave, as long as there is even one that wants to remain, even when there can be no separation, it's just the belief that you can, will keep your trip from ending.

We are all ONE. We cannot be separated from the One except in the believing it and we have bought into that belief, but it is time for that to end. If we are all one, we want to come home.

Did I start the flight or maybe plight of independence, and was I wrong? Perhaps, but am I liable for all the wrongs that have taken place since that day of extraction?

If that is so and it all has been my influence, then I have been made very powerful in deed, but this power is not of my making or design. There are those that would have power to control others and have used my name to try and divert the blame from them.

Music and singing were my first step in my separation, but only because I thought I was better then others, do not stop singing it is a true serenity in and of itself and but one way back to the peace we all once knew.

I am but one being, yet a part of the One as are all. If what I once did those billions of years back is the reason for another's personal and independent down fall, we all do have a very long path ahead of us and our collective rejoining with the One is sadly of a fare, fare distance.

If any or all of this seems in defense of what I have been subjected to or accused of having done; it is not at all.

As from the beginning the true memory of the before was not taken away from me as perhaps a part of the punishment, but in fact it is the one thing that I alone in this dimension have the certainty of knowing, and that is, that all things without exception are of the One and there can be **no** separation, and there will be inevitably a rejoining, all the rest of the pour souls can only dream and hope that there is any possibility of a better way of life and future.

I know that there is. And know that all in consciousness rejoin of the before.

It is very apparent that the many who did follow me and their memories wiped clean, were in fact far more severely punished then even I as the unknowing is by far more devastating then the exile itself.

If you let fear enter your mind, you are separating yourself from your own security, as what you fear most, has no substance beyond your mind, even the thought of death as an end is only true to the point of a transition beyond what we now deem as real.

The choice is always yours and it will remain that way until the perception of time and separation no longer exists.

God has not forsaken you. Your god has. If you are looking for God in a place, any single place that is at least a part of the problem as there is no place that the God is not.

You can blame the evil on the devil, but that is only because you will not take responsibility for your own thoughts and actions.

Nothing has changed even as from the before. If you follow of your own free will, who or what is to blame but one's self.

There are many, in fact most, that will blame anything or anyone but themselves for their dilemmas and look to their church, its pastor and elders for assistance and for most, it will cost.

Being one with the One Infinite Spirit is and never has been an issue. It is in fact an absolute, so where does the buying of forgiveness or that illusive ticket to heaven come from?

Power and greed for those that would benefit from these astronomical amounts. Again, God has no need of money. The essence of what God is is creative. Why would one have to charge when only a thought would create to perfection in abundance?

Will one be able to go to heaven and another not? Remember we ALL are a part of that One Creative Source and also have that inherent ability to create. It is the choice that makes the difference.

The awesome Holiness of those individuals within the physical consciousness of a nearly lost state of mind is their absolute belief in what they cannot see.

If you let fear enter your mind, you are separating yourself from your own security. For your fear is in the death, but death, as you understand it is in the physical form and in truth that is not where life is.

Listening to the one that has been deemed the bringer of all evil and speaking of human salvation is a foreign concept for most I am sure, and there will be those who do not trust my meaning or my message, but I have met with the one true loving God and I know God loves me, I also know that my own salvation is linked to yours.

There are those who truly believe that what they hold as truth is the only way to salvation, however, if you are holding onto a branch in a raging river with no way out, you need saving. But in the spiritual world, there are no lost souls.

The soul of humanity is one true part that cannot be lost, for it is the God essence that makes you a part of the One.

With time truly as a handicap, the physical universe is without any doubt awesome and even overwhelming.

I too am limited within time as well as the boundaries of this physical dimension, but not being physical or limited within a body I have traversed the expanses of the cosmos watching the wonders that creative power can achieve.

There is a diversity of independent life so phenomenal that it will stretch even the collective more over a single ones mind, as this heterogeneity spans all areas and dimensions that could be considered of the new to the outer most edges back to the very genesis of this dimension itself.

If there is anything to worship, it is the awe-inspiring totality of Infinite Creative Mind that encompasses all.

There are incarnations from every portion of your known and unknown vaults of the heavens that have incarnated within every part so the endless changes and mental abilities will continue as this experience continues.

As was said before, I have not experienced physical form as my being, therefore have not encountered that transition time between incarnations, which are however brief, a true glimpse of the before.

The one realization of certainty that may well evolve to a state of awareness to the consciousness of the Infinite may come more quickly to some than others, but the outcome is the same for all.

Have I been proclaimed the devil in other places? There is no place that conscious mind has not looked for a devil or something or someone to blame their ills on. It seems to be a natural conclusion especially to the religious mind.

The ones that believe in no god whatsoever are somewhat closer to the truth then most religions as responsibility must fall directly on themselves.

What dream scenarios have you put yourself into at this point of your existence?

There are those that cannot and will not accept even the thought of a situation such as has been presented here, but you have to admit that if there is an Infinite and loving God and I would hope that your God would be good and loving and not just to you, but to all.

You have heard some of these things in so many varied versions and nearly all from a physical standpoint and understanding, you must remember that the physical is merely a condition of mind, a dream, a scenario, an illusion. The only true reality is within the One Mind.

As for what is deemed bad, and not to minimize what bad and evil represents, but even in your existence you are forced to look at everything from perspective.

There are those that are willing to cut the short lives they now have entered in the name of family, country, or their god only because they believe in an ideology so strongly, their hoping their action will convince others of their way.

This form of persuasion is very deceiving as well as convincing, but never achieves for the one sacrificing only for the one instigating.

If humanity could get along regardless of beliefs, if only you let the others believe in theirs. It is when one demands that another do as they dictate that freedom no longer exist and there will be conflicts. That was proven fifteen billion years ago.

So you're wondering about hell, hum, your wondering where I'm living? Lets look at the word or place for a second, we're talking Hades, place of misery, the absolute of death, of fire and brimstone. Well if you really want to see fire and brimstone put yourself in the middle of a star at the instant it goes nova.

The beauty of that situation is without words of explanation, it has to be experienced and so you may have at one time in the past, it truly is beyond belief. Within this physical dimension it is close to one of the most devastating and destructive events that can be within a short period of time and probably one of the most beautiful.

It is the beginning of a whole new start because every piece of that physical stuff comes back to be something else whether it ends up as part of a tree, another planet an asteroid or living being, it comes back.

Should I mention the bible again? Was it inspired by the

Oneness of God and written by men? If there is nothing but God you may answer the question yourself, but if the self and personal gain, power, (ego) enters the equation, again the problems arise.

The truly significant, at least better known not to exclude the multitudes of those that have entered this dimension, chose to come and are not of the exiled but to experience what can only be encountered in this separated state.

Mohamed, Buddha, Jesus and many more even now and not from within this time period or planet have been showing a way to live and very few ever wrote it down.

If you ever say, the devil made me do it. Leave my name out of it. It was your decision. You are responsible for you.

The devil, the evil one, bringer of death, Satan.   This is a concept in the mind of those not wanting to take responsibility for their own actions.

The pain will pass.

The beauty will last forever.

Comments, remarks and observations

Comments, remarks and observations

Do we have a ? Guardian Angel

Guardian Angels

Dictated by Ken's Angel
Written down by Ken the Carpenter

There is a time in "everyone's" life when they know that they have been contacted by something that cannot be explained on the physical plane, as at most times it is a gentle nudging, at others it just could be a train wreck.

Each and every physical being is very much about his Fathers' business, whether they or anyone else may think or feel that way.

I am what most explain as a guardian Angel; my only responsibility is on a very personal level to only one being at any one time. I, of collective consciousness with independent consideration, reflection and contemplation, have never chosen to be of the physical plane, yet in total receptiveness with all emotions, situations and actions taken by the one we have arranged to watch over from before their moving within the physical.

At the point the physical dimension came to be there was immediate understanding that when entering within that realm, knowing of ones true nature is all but abolished with only a meager shadow even of hope. The reality that each and every act is a decision that individuals must and will make for themselves.

Without interference except to watch over with only subtle encouragements, but devoid of intervention we watched.

As the eons quickly dissolve into endless, but now linear perception of time, the ones now ensnared within this mind made dimension, during their stay is near to brutal, and was decided within Collective Conscious that a companion or guardian be assigned each entering this new and untried plane of existence.

When this physical dimension first came to be it was with truly an untried situation as never had there been any thought that separation from the One Mind was even possible. Unthinkable creativity was endlessly taking place within mind, but never with autonomy of mind entering the scenario. When at that moment it was first accomplished all of Infinite Mind stopped to observe.

With no way to anticipate, predict or foresee possible affects, monitoring and close scrutiny with constant analysis was thorough, systematic and meticulous. It was quickly observed that the independent consciousness that would enter this frightening position would lose any and all awareness of its natural state and or status and was truly alone and frightened.

Within such a terrifying state the illusion of separation would quickly dissolve away into the nothingness that it was, as the true creative consciousness would break free of the restricting shroud.

As those that entered would return to the One Mind the endless feelings of desperation, loneliness and fear were instantly spread throughout Mind, but to understand was impossible. It was said that the feelings of substance and time were near endless, yet short, and the concept of time was difficult to describe as infinite was all that had ever been known.

It was considered within the collective that any and all possible situations be played out within this new apparent, separated, alienated state, always realizing of the absolute return, but also that a companion or guardian be sent with each, with out exception, regardless of the scenario they chose to experience.

Eons quickly passed as tens of billions of separate circumstances, situations as individuals and as groups, even entire planets played out even more complex and diverse possibilities. Some were presented through contemplation, others totally unexpected and sporadic, but it was felt any and all should be finalized to completion regardless whether they near touched heaven or wallowed and floundered within the pit of hell. When complete they would never again be experienced in any way, as Mind would have full understanding of the agony and or ecstasy of all.

As the size and complexity of the individual brain increased an unexpected intensity of situations seemed on an endless roll of infinite potentialities. The power of independent creative thought was showing its true potentials of its source of being, but without the conscious connective ness with the One Mind as a self-determining and autonomous control of ones mind, could erratically spiral in every direction.

Was there to be an end of the seeming endless cycle, in particular on the down side? Although there was never any question as to the finial destination, the torturous agony of some seemed unnecessary, pointless and redundantly insane, but all without exception had entered with a clear mind choosing to participate in playing their part in whatever unforeseen situations may take place.

Could there be a judgment day for the evil activities and or instigators of this seeming pot of spoiled stew, or was it in fact still brewing to be looked back to and remembered in endless time as the dream that it truly is and was?

At certain times intervention from the guardians becomes necessary, as a part being played to a specific pre-contemplated possibility has an unforeseen tragedy or a situation occurs that deflects calculated trajectory into an unwanted end.

What is seen as a miracle takes place. But, in fact, only the script of that particular event is made to continue, even though that intersession in itself will change drastically what had taken place and a whole new series of events unfolds.

There are most certainly questions as to why are certain things allowed. In the language of your planet, why not? There is nothing but the infinite. There is no place, thing or being that is not of the Infinite. You must look at it as in your short existence and the busyness that fills your days, but in the Infinite there is no concept of end, all can last to its fulfillment and none of the Infinite has been used up.

It has been questioned by many especially on the spiritual path; if when true enlightenment finally is achieved, will I, as me, no longer exist when again rejoined to the One Consciousness?

Separation from the One is not possible, there is no returning as leaving cannot be achieved. This understanding is most important to all in order to live a life of true happiness.

The importance of ones self slowly starts to wane as they begin to understand when you are apparently in the state of separation and alone as in a dark and cold, frightening closet, verses at a wonderful party of many loving and playful friends with magnificent contemplation and agreement within all concepts.

The happiness amplifies while with them, but the feeling of ecstasy, joy, contentment and bliss is beyond contemplation to the human mind when the importance of ones self again realizes the magnitude of their connection to the allness of the One.

There are times that we hold you tightly in our arms as you struggle to clamber a seeming insurmountable obstacle or situation, but it is yours to complete or not.

As the incalculable situations have been closed as unnecessary, a somewhat new twist occurred within the ranks of the companions and guardians and the diverse ways of dealing with any one or more situations.

It had become very evident that although a situation with two or more individuals in an identical issue or circumstance, the outcome could be very different and the Guardian could only cause the perceptible difference.

When a plane falls from the air or a train leaves the track at high speed, all are devastated in some way, but there are always those few that walk away without a scratch. Why? Was that what was meant to be or a sporadic impulse response of the Guardian?

The Guardians are as freethinking as all of creation and have choices to make as do all without exception, but their only responsibility truly is that as companion or escort for their responsibility when their physical confines have been discarded and the soul is again free, to be the first thing that is seen whether it be the face of their mother or a cherished loved one.

The consciousness of that one liberated has been a part of and integrated within the limitations of that individual body so closely that on occasion to a point of total forgetfulness and disconnection as to their infinite being ness, that when leaving are in a state of such confusion and terror of disembodiment that there is the possibility of entering another's physical reality.

Not understanding the situation, as their beliefs in the physical had not allowed such a concept, to a point that when leaving it was as though they were in a bad dream, when in truth the very opposite was true, they had just left that dream or sometimes nightmare, regardless of what it may have been, but even with the Guardians at times it will occur.

It has been said that God knows nothing of pain, evil and suffering, as the concept of such is not possible within perfection, then how can one say that God is all knowing if he does not know all? Hurting, malevolence and anguish are conditions of the body, not mind; it is when the mind considers itself as part of the body is when the emotions of imperfections manifest as reality. God knows your pain as each are a part of the One Mind but understands this too came to pass, and will, as heaven is only a thought away.

The word God, or thought of an individual as the one and eternal, timeless head of state is only considered within the realm of a separated mental condition.

It is only a conception within the perception of that frightened mind and only because it does feel so alone.

There is no thing that is not a part of everything. The thought that this physical universe you live in now is immense and vast is only because it is viewed from within a physical concept, when within Mind there are no borders or end to anything that is considered, whether individual or within the collective. Eternal cannot be placed within time and space; it is the concept of time and space that separates one within their personal box.

If you place yourself within mind sitting on the outermost star of this physical cosmos, what will you see? It will be whatever you put there. If you want the stars to continue endlessly on, you will never come to the end of them, but if that is where you place heaven, that is what will appear as your concept of it or perhaps a black void of infinite nothingness. It is not the power of a telescope that expands the universe; it is the creativity of the mind.

I am right, my belief or religion is the one God, also believes? God is in my church? I know and feel I am right and that God is here agreeing with me. This is very much a mentality of separation as no one individual or group can separate themselves from another, it is not that God is equally within all things. There is nothing that is not God. As said before separation is not possible.

It is said by some that your physical existence is but an illusion or dream. They also say that all things are of mind. When within mind whether conscious or within a dream does the difference take place? There is no difference. It is only in the individual belief of aloneness and separation that the variation of diversity is created.

All things are of mind as a result, unreal? All things are of the One Mind therefore reality must be one and the same as what is felt to be illusion. Where can one make a distinction between the two?

Just the fact that one might think that there is a right mind and a wrong mind is in itself separation and consequently two independent powers and therefore conflict could occur. Again, not possible.

It is difficult perhaps to contemplate the devastations of greed, gluttony, hostilities to conflict, starvation, anger to rage, the agony of aloneness and the sorrow to endless grief in all matters, and all coming from what we feel as the Mind of God, but if it is not so, there must be two minds therefore two powers. This cannot be, and is not.

Within the physical realm all these thoughts, feelings and actions, are all linked to separation. If a thinking mind is doing anything it is curious, inquisitive and questioning of all things.

Within the collective there is truly no thought of wrongdoing and or evil, but as individual choice goes into place within an independent sphere, what is known as control from the outside is not possible as each and all are but a part in that all encompassing collective.

We know, see and feel the questions, WHY then? Why would God allow what is going on? It is not agreed to, contemplated on or in any way planned within a scheme or design of anything from a higher source of Consciousness, but what has taken place has been seen to encompass the needless waste of time within the physical and this too shall pass as time itself shall soon end for all and the endless Spiritual sojourn rolls on.

God is the essence of life itself, within, surrounding, all encompassing of all that there is. God is not a being. God is being. There is no thing that is not what God is. And still one will ask, why? What has caused and or allowed such negative?

As the individualized consciousness again realizes the restrictions, limitations and apparent separation from the One Mind, the understanding as to why, although the reasoning never moves far from insane, the knowing becomes clearer as said earlier; to be all knowing one must know all.

Time and space do not exist within creative Mind so although it seems and appears endless to those experiencing, infinity has not been depleted whatsoever.

Within the vast majority of western culture, Jesus is the icon and symbol for goodness and rightly so within the perspective of understanding of most, when in truth he did come with an agenda, not to save the world of their sins, but to show that life within this realm could be lived fully and joyously. what most consider as life in the physical, truly is not, In the physical, death seems the final destination and end of life, but is from the before and cannot be destroyed.

As said earlier there is no situation, circumstance or scenario that will not be contemplated within mind as to a possibility and each must be carried out to completion. The independent consciousness that has agreed upon whatever was assigned has and will, while within the progression and course of action of its task within the physical, at times reject continuation of its allocated undertaking and or assignment and is then subtly and delicately nudged on to its conclusion.

Would these guardians be mistaken for, what is known as the dark side or fallen angel? Of that there is no doubt, but their situation is no different then the one standing beside Jesus, Buda, Hitler or you, it is but to close the book on all that is deemed not necessary.

Your human intellect is so limited as all that can be perceived is from a linier perspective.

Endless or infinite is not at all within the realm of a straight line of events so is impossible to correlate or fit the puzzle parts together as some have not yet been formed to their completion.

Judgment of any kind within the life span in the physical is impossible as the matured intelligence of an individual is truly so very short that any culmination of accurate conclusion is at best fragmented. Every book in your world read and remembered by one individual would not give them the ability to create life.

Life cannot be created. Regardless of intelligence, intellect or even god like abilities, life without exception is of the in the before the beginning. God is what life is and god is and has always been complete and cannot be added to or depleted from, as perfection is without fault or blemish.

Perfection remains infinite even without conscious thought, but to apply the precept within ones lifetime is what god is, in action within this dimension.

It has been said by many as well as within literally all those proclaiming that their way is where it's at, they know there are teachers of the spiritual way and they have most of them. They are wrong about having most of them, but all in their circle are absolutely teachers, what nearly all do not realize is that there is no other then what is the spiritual way, as all have life so are of God and about his work.

It cannot be stressed enough. **Judge not!** When judgment enters the mind separation again shows its ugly and frightening side. The one judging again enters their world of fear and aloneness while the one being judged knows nothing of their being judged and continues on in innocence.

This narrative has been contemplated seriously within Mind, as without reservation the precept of wrongdoing seems justified. Wrong is wrong without exception, then how can this be defensible.

On your level of understanding and within your appeared separated state it is near impossible. The closest one can come is as watching the events on a screen with only actors playing out the parts with no reality what so ever involved.

My child, my mother, father, my friend, all that I loved. What of them? It was not wrong what happened to them?

You must stop for a moment and take a deep breath and feel the life that is within you. That life is God.

The life that was in your loved one was also none other then God itself experiencing what must be completed and you were at his side as a willing participant.

What most do not realize is that they are playing the major and focal role within the scenario, their loved one has returned to their origin of being and is now connected with you in mind so much closer then can be contemplated.

"I want them in my arms," You say. They are, and forever will be as the part that has been played has been recorded within the finalized records.

This is not fair. This is obscene. How can this be justified?

The feeling of unfair, obscenity and the need for justification again separate one from the truth. You were playing a part at the right hand of God and did it to completion. All of Infinite Mind thanks you. If it were a scene of despair and anguish, you are especially thanked for taking the role, as never again will that exact part be required.

Many may ask, how can some people be or at least act or respond as though everything is just fine, there is no war, no fear, no pain or anguish.

In truth, all that is experienced is within mind. The reality of anything is totally within the perspective of each individual. There are those that have transcended the nightmares that are created by others and do not take on another's fears. Reality is what you separately believe in isolation.

The possibility of a war being waged all around one and they have no awareness of it whatsoever is entirely possible.

The entire physical dimension is but an experience in mind. If all is but a part of the one Mind then how can an individual ignore it?

One must remember that time and space also are but an occurrence within the physical dimension.

A person does not have to be meditating, isolated in a cave, high in the Himalayas to transcend into peace and love. For those that do not believe this possible, it will not be so, but for an enlightened few it is everyday life.

This does not have anything to do with them not caring, indifference or aloofness or in feeling superior and coldness for another, although many see them and treat them that way, the very opposite is truth as they will always be showing love and peace without judgment or prejudice. It is they that give light and hope for the entire race. Judge them not as their Infinite sojourns did not just begin and it is their time.

Without exception, when leaving this physical plane you are again welcomed home. Your thoughts of all that has occurred while within the physical have been instantly cleared from your mind and an unequivocal knowing of peace and love permeates and encapsulates your entire being with no feelings of separation or aloneness possible.

For some this experience may be needed for only a short period as others may melt themselves within the clouds of love and not remembering for eons.

When this short sojourn has finalized, your guardian, and constant companion will again connect with you face to face so to categorize your file within the library of Mind.

God will bless you and keep you safe within his arms, forever.

Comments, remarks and observations

If there was a
Beginning

there had to be,

In the before the Beginning

In the BEFORE the BEGINNING

By Ken, The Carpenter with help

There was a darkness that was so absolute that life as we know it, could in no way exist.

There were no stars in the sky, there was no sky so to say, and there was only darkness. A darkness that is beyond what the mind of man could ever comprehend. There was no feeling of fear, no animosity, no feeling of loneliness. Only an infinity of absolute and total nothingness, an emptiness of never having been, or even thought of. The beginning and the end on the point of a pin. Nothing on this what we call a physical plain for a physical dimension, in fact, as of yet did not exist.

For one millisecond there was a single flash of light. Then again came the blackness, the infinite and absolute nothing. There seemed to be a change. Though how could there be a change in nothingness? Even though there seemed to be. Then came a vibration, or was it a feeling? Yes, it was such a total and incomprehensible feeling, that of an Infinite and Absolute Power.

A stimulating yet never before felt changes in Thought. For this thinking Power was not, nor had it ever been physical. Even though there was that feeling of change, as that of the mind of a Creator in an untried and uncertain beginning. And yet it was, as though billions of creative minds with undreamed of thoughts and dreams, were about to burst free from singularity of thought.

Was this the Absolute Thinker, One Mind, Creative Thought Source?

Was the Thought of **CREATION HAPPENING?**

As this creative thinking was going on, the black void of nothingness was occasionally being interrupted, with a web like lightning, sporadic and without any order, appearing from apparently nowhere.

Then again that feeling. Almost an anticipation of a change. A change in what? The blackness had fallen back to its absolute. But now the darkness, the seeming and overwhelming nothingness appeared even more intense.

The powerful and untried feeling of change and growth were awe-inspiring.

Then the sound of a voice that seemed to come from nowhere, or was it from everywhere? It was the first sound that had ever been. At the exact instant that the voice sounded, saying

"I AM," a brilliant flash of light filled all of Infinity with one exploding burst. That one unimaginable flash vibrated and rippled to the very center of the Mind and Soul of the Creative Thinker Itself. It was gone as quickly as it had come. Again the thick and intense darkness.

For only a moment, the darkness seemed to have a rolling web cloud affect with sporadic lightning entangled within it.

Then again, the blackness. The ultimate of darkness. That point in which even the soul has no seeming access. The feeling of no feeling or being. Then a small crackle and flash.

Then came the feeling of a Mind that had to burst into existence. Again, the Voice, the sound that filled all of infinity from beginning to beginning and on. The sound rebounded in and through any and all dimensions and areas of thought. It was though a chorus of billions upon billions was calling out. Yet it was one voice.

I AM MORE. As the sound was booming out, the blast of creation exploded into a new untried physical dimension.

What is a physical dimension? What is physical???

The absolute blackness and total void of nothingness is becoming filled with this stuff. Fill? What to fill? What stuff? We are talking Infinity, no beginning, and no end.

So here again we are moving beyond the realm of the physical mind. Beyond the understanding or comprehension of the finite, this cannot be denied.

Was all of this coming from one spot in this now physical manifestation? Was it just materializing at the point of it's now existence? Did it begin total and complete? Was it going on to grow and change? What possible reason could there be that this was happening? What was it coming from?

To what end? Would there be an end? Or was this new arrival as infinite as the dimension it was moving into and from? Could there be life in it? If it was to grow, it must have Life.

Where was it all coming from? Was it all oozing out of a pinhole fracture in another dimension wall? If this is so, again to what end? Were there other areas of the thinking process to try? Was there One Mind in charge of what was going on? Was there a collective thought process? Was there?? Was there???

Why do we ask why, I AM? Why? How? From what? From Where? What is the reason that I AM? Now as for the story these questions are totally irrelevant. For I AM NOT yet physical, for now there is only a physical matter becoming a physical universe. Is there a plan? Is there only a random sequence of ongoing situations, that are causing thought to happen, to create the ongoing change that was and is going on in all we see as a universe of solid matter?

If thought was and is a factor, then there was in fact a thing we may call creation. You may believe anything you so desire. Even if it is only true from your point of view. As for me that is fine. Just fine.

As the physical manifestation is spreading infinitely further out into the newly acquired areas of growth, there seems almost a sense of wonder and other new, and unfelt, untried feelings. Shall we say emotions?

For the first time, there was a first time. A feeling of a beginning.

In this new dimension, new things could start.

Would they have an end?

What type of an end? What would it end to? Where would it go?

Would this new whatever, go back to the point before the I AM? Will this universe become as eternal and infinite as in the before the beginning?

Would it in fact go back to what in truth it seems not to be, the non-physical manifestation of thought.

As this mighty onrush seems to slow and cool, a somewhat strange yet understandable change starts taking place.

All this materialized stuff started clinging together. Some large, some small and some very large balls or spheres that seemed to defy any physical law. That is if, there are any absolute this or that to anything in this incomprehensible physical dimension.

The larger masses started taking on the dominant roll, as this strange new power of gravitation seemed to take hold of everything. This too, was all very new and untried. This new manifested dimensional universe seemed to expand and grow.

The creative and expressive consciousness that had thought this into being, has by now, so to say, caught up and was moving on to more creative ways to express.

The universe was ablaze, almost the total opposite of the before. Even the thought pattern seemed to have changed.

Their invention was with unlimited possibilities and unto now undreamed of dreams.

The creative thought deluge seems to be stretching out to the far reaches of what is now space and newly developed solar systems. The all-encompassing oneness of thought seems to be filtering off into different areas and lines of independent thinking and creativity.

Even though there is no feeling of separation or attitude of independence, there are obviously pockets of individualized and seemingly personal creativeness. That is in no way separate from the Creative Power Source, for Creative Power Source of what we call First Thought continues only to spread itself in further and ever more creative ways. Time and space have no definition to that of which it it has created.

There seemed to be a slowing, almost a hesitation or maybe somewhat of a regrouping of thought. There in a few small groups of what we now call solar systems was the feeling that a seed had been planted. It was as though the rest of the limitless rumbling on of creation seemed to stop and look back and watch and wait.

What would come of this new creation? This individualized consciousness assuming the roll of an almost independent entity. Separate and apart from the one.

Was there perhaps another reason for this newcomer? Everything was new and untried.

There seemed to be a change in the flow of conscious thought, through this strange yet somehow beautiful manifestation. It was somewhat permanently rooted to one place. Would or could this create anew and of itself.

This was of the new creation. Even the new was of the before. All things were manifestations of the original thought, yet individualized and with creative choices.

As thought is poured into the new seed of creation a trunk and branches begin to appear and grow, larger and ever larger they become. Now as the creative thinking flows through and is developing, a very unnatural thought manifests. Instead of the infinite and timeless eternal, the thought was where would this one expression extend?

How could it change? How could it expand without it itself covering an entire globe?

As billions upon billions of our now newly individualized and somewhat independent free thinking personalities seemed to pause from their creative activities to look to the new and growing life form, new creative mental images and thoughts were abounding in and through the allness of Mind. What was it exactly? What is it we have here? Was it a, so to say, life form at all or was it in fact but an expression of an independently creative thought.

As our tree grew and grew and grew, the size seemed to be gaining little and no expression of itself except to that of the size only.

There seemed to be a thought, no, a need to move on with this creation and other ways to express.

Express, that was it. To express as of the before, to create of the self, to extend and expand on and on and on. To continue on to the infinite. If not as of the first, as the expansion of the same.

But again the action at hand was to create and move on. Move on, well if the first seed was planted of creative thought and now second seed and more were on tree, second seed then must be planted of the creation.

To in fact achieve any advancement or continuity was to create of ones self. Life is. Life is of the before. It is the animator of the dream and thought. The thought is the designer.

All of the POWER or SOURCE of the allness was of but ONE MIND. There is nothing that is separate. There was no aloneness. For all that there was and is has the CREATIVE SOURCE flowing in, through, and around each and every cell and atom of existence to the top branch of our first and most mighty tree.

If tree was to create of itself and plant it's own seeds, we are at a point of somewhat a design dilemma within creative thought. HOW? With what? Where? What were seeds anyway? At that instant a beautiful flower appeared and within this flower seeds formed with a genetic and molecular structure identical to that of the original design thought. For to now this was instantly and easily manifested through creative Mind.

But now the thought came, only one flower one seed, one time. Then there would be two. Why not a million seeds? More and More? But then, would all the millions upon millions of seeds fall in this one small spot? How could this seed transport itself off to other areas?

Could, would they roll? Could they fly? Could they be carried? Carried by what? How? Where? And why would this whatever carry a seed anywhere and plant it just so tree could extend its territory? But again, where is or what is the vehicle?

Again the allness of infinity and the MIND, the in the before the beginning seemed to slow and take careful thought.

There was another relatively small planet across what we may see as infinite and timeless space from our tree. But, in thought there is no conception of what may be mistakenly taken as time and or space in the dimension of thought and creativity, for the Mind of the CREATOR is infinite and without boundaries or limitations. For even though diversified and with limitless options and opinions, all was as one; as had always been and would always be.

But, now as for the distance to this new planet, it was many millions upon billions of light years across what we see as impossible space with countless super giant masses and innumerable billions of Galaxies. Collective MIND and the oneness of thought was in fact there, to witness, comprehend, and see an, as to now untried creation.

On this landmass was something moving, unsupported and with independent motion as of an individualize and seemingly separate entity, but there seemed to be no reason for it. But, what is reason? Is it not but relating back to what is or has been tried? Where there is no comparison and from the perspective of creative thought, reason does not necessarily fall into the area of need or desire. But, here was a mobile unit.

With MIND moving us back to tree and its' as yet unsolved dilemma of mobile seeds, an infinitely cooperative response burst forth a mighty wind and so scattered all the seeds in every direction and area, along with a very large percent of the branches and a few remaining buds. You might say tree was stripped clean of its apparent method of procreation.

There it stood cold and bare. As for now has tree done its work? Has its destiny been fulfilled? Was it only first, and now of no more good or significant to anything?

Would it, in fact just disappear back into the mind of the Creator from where it had been conceived? If so, had it in fact ever been, or was it only the manifestation of thought?

Again, if that to is so, what are the seeds? Are they a part of the original thought or are they a part of tree and not of the Creator? There was NOTHING, NOTHING before the first physical creative thought of I AM MORE. NOTHING. All things then must in fact, be of the original I AM.

As the wind blew, seeds had found spots under stones and while resting there and with no real thought, that is, as we could perceive it, waited. The winds were blowing up wonderfully beautiful and refreshing rain clouds which were but a part of an on going pattern in this new physical dimension of need, desire, and survival of materialized thought.

As the mind works, the more we dream and think. The more we dream and we think, things start to happen.

When the thinking and the dreaming are going on, all things are first time prototypes. The excitement of creating as mind was working, would be an emotion beyond even that of the dream, for even the feeling of emotion was new.

As countless billions of independent and individualized creative thinking processes are going on, they are totally interconnected. The outcome would be at a point each unique and yet from the same bases of thought and the basic fundamental principles flowing through the only conduit of MIND.

There is a barrage of thought, design and creation.

Practice, practice, practice. There was some designs that went smaller and smaller and smaller while others went to the other side of the scale and their large sizes seemed to go beyond any real practical reason.

Then again, what is reason? Why would there be any reason to question new and untried, if the creating is in fact going on in a what you might call, practice mode.

As the individualized creative thought is in no doubt interconnected, the creative outcome would cover the span of the spectrum to the degree of quantity of specific thought patterns concentrating within any one creative field or area specifically within the new physical dimension.

Tree was standing there, the absolute of individualized creativity. Was it still alive? What was alive at this point? Standing tall yes but stripped clean. The question is, will it be able to reproduce itself or had that already happened when the seeds left for parts unknown?

As time moved on, TIME, what is time? How can time be comprehended in MIND? That is of forever? There is no beginning of creative Mind. This is only a new and untried area of consciousness in which to expand.

Seed was not a tree. Yet, it was putting down a feeler to find what it needed to grow and stay alive. For it was in fact very separate and totally on it's own from original tree. Even though it had all the genetic outlines and characteristics of number one.

As time moved on, all the seeds began to grow and produce seeds and they would grow and produce seeds and on and on and on, till they were literally covering the planet.

Was Mind taking all this in and contemplating perhaps what the end result might be? Or was Mind just watching and letting tree be? The growth and expansion happened.

Infinite Creative Mind couldn't even start to comprehend an end result. Beginning and ending was not a part of its' make-up.

Without this in consciousness, it would not create within that premise. With this thought, new plans were being molded and tried within mind before any type of manifestation came to be.

The all ness of Infinite Mind was without any judgment or preference to any one expression of conscious thought. Except, to the fact that all things were in fact a part of the whole. So if there could be any type of what we could comprehend as caring, it would be in the way of growth.

The individualized creative thought source of tree traveled off through the conduit of Mind, the ever expanding arena of this physical dimension, to experience through the dimensional sources, newly tried areas of physical life, demonstrated by other creative segments of mind.

There is no replacing being a part of the new and untried, to gain not only through, but also as the experiment. There could be no other logical reason for the dimension at all.

As the experience moved through its course in time and the intended or the by chance took place, the information and experience took its toll, for it was above all else with no limitation in any form of thought or in creativity.

The creative consciousness of tree escaped out of this life form in the far off and distant galaxy of space and was instantly back at tree with so many new and different ideas and concepts, that the process of creating seemed to roll out over the lands and the water. Colors and shapes came together with strange and yet beautiful blends. There were as though many different family types, some unrecognizable to each other yet the same, linked to a genetic chain.

The families grew in size and number. As time moved on, some of the members seemed to change or evolve. Was this evolution taking place by chance and, or happenstance? Or were they being changed and altered as nesting and eating habits were developed, as adapting to terrains and climates became a major part of survival.

Was this evolution at all? I say yes! Was this an evolving through need and almost by chance? If the changes didn't take place, would the breed have died out? Think of this.

Was it a creative upgrading of the species to in fact make surviving less a struggle, to all but guarantee the continuation of life with a bit more ease.

Is there an individualized independently thinking creative source within each and every manifested thing that has appeared on the physical plain? Is this dimension a classroom to try and better understand the allness of the one, the personal individuality's of the allness?

Living creatures were beginning to fill the lands and the waters were surging with life. A conscious awareness or at the least a collective consciousness, seemed to keep the countless many varied species within the confines of their own genetic types, as to continue the breed.

There seemed to be less then complete freedom as to habitat and most degrees and or situations in the day-by-day survival of the single unit. Survival of the breed was first and foremost.

Time was passing so very quickly and the changes were coming and then changing again and again, to the point that the original was in truth an original. For very few had or even could stay the same, in order to survive in the many different and also changing landscape and conditions that had very much taken over the mentality of the creatures. Survival was the one, the only one desire. There was no room or time for much else. For if they were not eating, they were busy tying not to be eaten.

As the creative individualities in conscious awareness of the in the before the beginning, surveyed the situation and conditions that seemed to trap them when inhabiting the physical dimension, they decided to try a little different approach, with a less limited arena for survival and with a much broader spectrum.

It would be aware that it was not only of, but it was the individualized creative mental source of itself.

Not limited if so desired in the area of mental capacities, but to have a conscious awareness of themselves and others around them and in fact of everything from the smallest to the most distant and largest and or any area in or around anything.

Mind was contemplating this new avenue in which to express. Not as an onlooker, but to be consciously integrated within the creation. Not to say, I will watch over this one more carefully, or to be helping it. To in fact, be it.

To create a new and as to now untried. It would be total and complete pure and perfect. It would be the very ultimate of creation: to this point, in this delightful new creative theater, this physical dimension.

While planning and design was taking place, and interest of infinite proportions was in itself causing the all ness of Collective Mind, to again, seemingly slow the out push of the on going of creation. The Oneness truly was of the in the before the beginning. The thought was not of how this new and unthought-of creation would be put together, or of what the I.Q. might be or would it be the biggest and best with untold beauty.

The thought was of the integrating of an Individualized part of the Infinite Creative Source itself as a part of the physical experience.

(If I may try) To instead of watching a motion picture on a screen so to say, to become one of the caricatures in the drama. What would the outcome be? There was no way to anticipate any type of a conclusion. For the caricature would no longer be somewhat as a puppet. It would in and of itself be the creator of it's own being. This individualized portion of the Creative Source would be wrapping itself within the confines of a physical frame.

Would this Creator confine itself to a point of entrapment within this frame? Would it in fact also seclude itself of communications with the allness of Collective Mind? Not likely, for it was creating only new experiences to learn from, to better understand itself. It was not, nor could it separate itself from the One Source for there was nothing else but the One.

The minutes, the days, the centuries flew by and the experience of interaction with nature and all of creation became as one family, through the eyes and independent mind of this one being moving about the planet watching the evolution of plant and animal unfold as the two seemed to merge and within themselves become as but one.

The expansion and preservation of the different species as independent families, started to become somewhat of a focal point. The sometimes struggle to survive as an individual independent of the family or group was not the goal or even a possibility in the game of survival.

As the numbers of varied species continued to expand, the families grew to a point of covering even different continents. It seemed obvious, yet not an absolute, that power was a deciding factor in independence and procreating of the family and species in general.

By this time the creator in physical manifestation as a single and independent one of a kind, **HUMAN**, was in communication with all other independent creators with their personal and separate dreams through out the endless and infinite cosmos.

This one and only physical being on this one small planet looked on at the private lives and obvious tenderness in close families and it gave the on-looker the feeling of separation and aloneness.

To this first time and before untried creator within the physical realm the sensation was new and in no way desirable.

Yet, with all of the many creatures and the communication there was in fact that one on one closeness that did not fulfill a physical yearning when without a companion

What is one to do? As for creative ability there were no limitations.

As for a companion????????

I AM A CREATOR.

I am not all there is of what is known as the ONE. I am but one minute and almost undetectable segment in the body of the all ness, but I AM A CREATOR of my own physical BEING, and dreams. I have created this world and all that is in it. As for me it is very good.

Now that I have put me here, I will deal with it. These FEELINGS, what are they? These DREAMS why are they? EMOTIONS, from where have they come?

I know that I AM infinite, I AM of the in the before the beginning. I AM of the conception of this dimension, for my thoughts are now physical. I AM now dwelling within the creation of my thought and dream. I AM not a captive of this form; I AM a part of it, and it of me.

Yet, there is a physical calling for a physical partner and companionship.

Now that I too am one with the other creatures, the understanding for family and YES, I will even say NEED as a physical being, is to belong, expand and be needed. These alone seem to be more compelling even than the seemingly inherent demands for personal survival within this consciousness.

As conscious thought expands almost as a wave moving out over the endless confines of space, companion is the focus of thought. The emotion of the thought of physical companionship is to now without comparison even in Mind. As to now, the collective consciousness of all that there is and ever was in the area of in the before the beginning where all thought did in fact begin and still was, except for this new illusion of separation as individuals in the physical dimension, could not be fairly or even coherently considered as it was in no way an issue.

But here was this One of a kind, standing alone, at least as a specie there was no other.

As this creative dream of creation at this specific point of time in space was in fact of the ONE alone standing, facing out to the unbelievably beautiful and infinite physical cosmos.

With eyes, heart and mind wide open contemplating and visualizing the dream of a partner and co-creator. It could be no less, or no more. It had to be as all other things were before it, of the creator itself. As the visions swirled within the creative mind, a brightness began to envelope the being.

As the brilliance seemed to begin to spin and whirl, the figure within became seemingly part of the light itself, and then only a shadow would appear.

It was as though a change would come and then go and then another and another, then a slowing, or was it slowing? No, it was apparently filling the area that was once the light. For creative thought was again becoming physical.

Was a metamorphoses taking place from within original being.

The pulsating and swirling light continues. It seems to extend around the being and to somewhat radiate, in a subtle and also melodious aura. The rotation of the light almost as a cocoon has enveloped its occupant.

Our Being is there, but there are no apparent features penetrating the density and intensity of this marvel in creative thought in action. For this time our Creative being was in fact truly creating for the first time of itself as and in this physical realm.

Are we watching, shall we say, re-creation or maybe another form or method of creative evolution taking place?

Are we seeing for the first time, the infiltration or merging or even perhaps a joining of another individualized creator within the dream of another's as of now, personal creation?

As the overwhelming drama of an unknown situation transpires and with an almost negative turmoil, yet again that feeling of emotion seems to weigh strongly within the decision.

For now emotion has been a prevailing and most powerful instigating factor for what is taking place within this paradox. This would be the first time that any decision or agreement had been made by two minds on a single course of action in a personal nature.

As from the beginning of the physical dimension the independent creative sections or segments of the One Mind that for some reason move into the creative mode and out into this newly formed cosmos had been to a degree working in and of oneself.

For the dimension of solid was new and as of all new things one seems to have to work alone till there becomes an understanding of what at least some of the affects that will come when moving into that unknown.

Now as for our One and to now alone creative being on this small and wondrous world, a creative decision of a most meaningful and in fact infinite magnitude was in the arena and the final outcome was in no way preordained or an absolute.

There was that innermost part of the all ness of all things that had been and always would be a part of all.   With this in mind and as the almost or seeming state of ferocity within the area began to settle, the intense light was almost wrapping tighter around this drama and yet it seemed to be increasing in size.

Then the light all but went away and a warm soothing glow was left, wrapped around somewhat of a cloud or fog that the being was engulfed in. There was a change, maybe not at first glance, but yes there was.

As the onlookers were all very much enraptured, our creative being was becoming wider, not fatter, wider.

There were two distinct bodies: almost as if pushing each other apart. For either there was still a matter of control as we might see it or the equality and separate design of the creative part and container of the brain were not as yet complete.

A flash of light that could be compared only with the first burst, which brought this dimension into being, seemed to paralyze all motion on the planet.

This burst of energy came from the outside, down into the circle of decision almost as a fireball. It was as though there had been a siphoning off of a bit of all that had to now been created and some that was only still in thought.

Apparently this finalized the decision, for as the force exploded into the scene there were two distinct and separate beings standing face to face with both hands still tightly clasping the hands of the other being.

Were they separate? Were they still connected or were they clinging to each other for support?

As they looked into each other eyes, there was indeed a communication of minds. There was no way to know which was the original creative being, for neither was as the one that had been.

The hands fell apart and the one occupying the position of first human took a few steps back and looked at the other with a feeling that can in no way be put into words.

He knelt to one knee with his arms extended out over his head and looked up with his eyes to the infinite cosmos. His mind moving out, and within, wanting to engulf the allness of

Creative Source to the very soul of creative mind. For again the true knowing of oneness was within him.

There had seemed to be for a period of time that feeling of aloneness while in this physical dimension, even though there was at no time any lack or even feeling of withholding of communication from within the body of the allness of Creative Source.

Perhaps being with all the animals and yet not one of them had been the final factor in the development of Human emotion and the desire for a companion and mate.

During this time of contemplation and fulfillment of mind and soul in who we now know as first man, but now our new being, even though being able to know the thoughts and have the feelings flood through her body and mind could in no way understand them.

This new being was a first timer on the physical plain. This body was new and very much of an unreal and unknown combination and collection of almost ridiculous emotions, nerves, and feelings.

She had just witnessed such a blessing and thanksgiving, that no one or group of independent creators had ever experienced or thought of. Even of in the before.

Yet, in her mind, she knew that at any instant of any instant, First Being, now man, could have left all that it had created and gone back to as it had always been and would in fact always be.

Even though living within and being not only apart of, but being a Creator of it all, he had chose to not only stay, but to expand the experience. For this was becoming much more interesting.

Was the new being female, a part of first being? Or was she in fact an independent?

There were none that were separate from the allness of first Source.

The allness of first thought of the in the before the beginning was Absolute, Infinite, and Eternal.

All were with independent and personal thoughts and creative abilities, so were in fact, what you might say, separate. Also being able to create of their own free will to that point of which they so desired.

Woman, now knowing that she was truly a being in and of herself.

Yes, a part of first being, but also a new life form, separate and independent from in mind and thought and yet still as a part of, through the allness.

She took a step or two back from the man facing her, and knew in her mind that he had brought the dream and vision of what she was in this physical form into manifestation.

There was the body of a dream and the mind of an independent soul.

Was this going to work as a companion and mate?

There seemed to be a definite possibility for differences of opinion. What we now have are two individual and unlimited creative parts of the One Mind now in separate bodies on the same planet.

The melding of the two minds was as though there were but one, for they were both very willing participants of this first time, and very emotional experiment.

For first being, (man) the realization of mutual and combined creativity again overflowed him with a very warm and tingly and before now unfelt feeling of emotion.

Dreams now could be viewed from different points, maybe not even created, but just felt. Perhaps even rationalized to the point of what was seen as perfection at that one point of mutual consent. This was wonderful. One on one. No master, no subordinate. Only one creative activity within the combined and agreed on purpose and final goal.

As the two of them went on from day to day doing what ever it was they felt they wanted to do, the bonding of their thoughts and of their bodies and their souls became ever closer.

They had become as one again, even as in the before, their feelings and desires were not always the same.

However, their independent thoughts and abilities did enhance and thrust on the ever on-going of what could not be stopped. Creation.

All things that had not been tried or made were in fact creating.

The new concept to both, but mostly to the woman, was time. For before entering this new way of living there was no time, not even a concept of it, for eternal, infinite, that was it.

Now there was a feeling and also the witnessing of beginning and ending.

There was new life coming into the world as newly formed creatures. The obvious result of survival was a constant degree for wondering.

For as the bodies of some of the creatures would seemingly get weaker as a period of time would go by, it appeared to Man and Woman that this physical dimension was in fact a universe of matter that could be formed into any shape, or even that matter would take the form of what ever thought the creator would put into it.

Was this universe then a reality? Or was it but the whim of a creative thinking source. Man, Woman, they were in fact the manifestation of but a dream.

Man had been on this small planet for what would be known in time as many, many centuries and as a distinct being and had become even stronger and in a physical sense wiser in the ways of this dimension and planet

Woman was relatively new on the scene and extremely active in this now physical nature or natural world. It was a wonderful creative playground.

As the woman was becoming very involved with the creatures and the plant life, she was taking careful notice that these plants and animals did in fact have a life of their own as individuals.

They were very much a part of the physical dimension, for they were but an assembly of matter particles. They were absolutely alive from the animation of the life giving thought from their creator; first being.

As time went by, She watched the tiny seeds form in and on the trees and other plants. She also began to acquire a distinct interest in how the pollination of the plant life was taking place.

In the animal world, there too was a distinct process of continuation of the species and or family. Only here there seemed to be an almost consent between the male and female of the same species or a familiarizing and an understanding between them. For the family to grow and continue, it did in fact take both of them.

It was in fact a process that took more than one. It did take what is known now as a male and or female to transfer or plant a seed and then for that seed to grow until it too could reproduce in the same manner. Another offspring from the combined and only manner for continuation on their world.

As the female being, watched and contemplated this method of the process of creation from within the physical realm, she began to look at herself and try to visualize and better understand how or even if, she too would have an offspring and build a family.

Am I a part of a species or am I just this being that I am?

The creative glow that had been a part of the process of her entering this body and the physical world was still surrounding her.

Almost a protective barrier from the outside world.

Am I a part of this new creation? Have I now become a combination of the creative source of the in the before and of the here and now? Am I an independent and individualized part of the all ness? Manifested here and on this planet? Or as part of a dream that has in fact no reality in it, as me?

I Am. And I know that I Am.

Are we a part of this world, and then at the mercy of the conditions that seem to take over when joining in and consciously taking part?

From observing all that is on the planet, and in the manner too which they participate, it is an absolute.

What is seen here is only the survival of the specie. Much less as an individual.

Is there a point at which the creative I AM and this new form are not one and the same? Is this new and beautiful creation, but a vehicle for my true self, the I AM, that is of the before?

If we should so desire to obligate and or commit to an entire specie such as ourselves, will we not only surrender the body, but also the mind to that point to where it would seem that what is as observed in the natural order of nature, would in fact take over as instinct to procreate and the overwhelming force to survive, at all cost?

I am a new being in and of myself, yet I know that I Am of a far greater creative source.

I am an individualized Being and as for now have entered this body with my consciousness, and am totally integrated within it to that point to which the body would surely not continue to function or even exist as a living thing if in fact I as consciousness would leave this manifestation that I now am.

With all of this in mind, and with constant communication with the allness of creative thought, we, the two and only beings of our type here on this planet have decided after tremendous contemplation and observation of many countless generations of the innumerable species, that we will become a most glorious and unique of all that has life as to now in this physical dimension.

My most wonderful companion and partner and I will become mates in the physical process to which this procreating can continue on as an independent and on going specie.

The individualized and single creator of this particular world has agreed that as the creation of the many different and varied types of plants, and also the many thousands of unique and beautiful animals was the manifestation of his one dream.

It would be mine to decide upon what and how that our particular family would manifest.

I alone have decided that I shall develop this new being of my own body and now become the female and carrier of this creation.

The first being of this world as my constant companion and ever-cherished mate will now become the male, and as from the very first plant the seed.

I (woman) have decided that we will go to the place of the first seed. To where mighty tree grew from that one seed. At this most holy of places is where the first seed for a new race of beings as and from the physical again will be planted.

As man and woman laid down under the giant and again great tree, there was still the shimmering glow on and around it that had been from its created beginning.

There was a special feeling being at this place. For there was here a knowing of the infinite and of the finite.

This was the one and only spot on this planet worthy of this first time and never before enactment of creation solely as a physical being.

As with tree, man and woman too were enshrouded within the creative glow in and of themselves.

While they were communicating and contemplating on what was about to become the beginning, of not only their family, but as they had witnessed in all of the physical creation this one act would in fact start a new specie.

In their hearts there was that knowing of the fact, that it would be good. With nothing but love for each other, this feeling of companionship and caring for another was without comparison.

As first man and first woman were acquainting themselves, there were some new strange and to now unknown feelings taking over their emotions.

They looked into each other's eyes and could feel that in their minds that they had given and released their bodies to this new creative goal.

For as of now between the two of them there was no stopping the act of procreation as there seemed even to them that over powering and never before felt unique glow within themselves.

As Man released his seed to Woman to combine with and reproduce a like being, the woman not only knew that a new life had been planted, but could sense that this seed had been directed by an independent consciousness of which and in fact this new being would become.

Our offspring will be as we are. We are very much separate in body, and yet cannot extend the family without becoming as one.

When the seed has been planted an individual creative independent consciousness which is of the allness will receive the mind, the body will take on the genetic features of both that partake in the creative ritual of life.

In this manner all of this specie will in fact never be exact. They will have identities and personal independent features that no other will claim as theirs.

Each and every one will become as another part of that absolute and infinite source of the allness of the in the before.

For there is nothing else. I, and all else are of the ONE.

I will allow the already tried and proven in the natural way of things, as to the development and proper timing for our new offspring to join us on this wondrous world.

This new being will, in the physical, be in this world, but as a living knowing consciousness, not of it, for it's true being and life source will be infinite and eternal and inhabit this body of it's choice only as long as is needed and or wanted.

The being is of the consciousness of the all ness and not of the physical make-up of this dimension. For we have observed that the process and continuity of having a physical form is not without risk.

We know this dimension is but the manifestation and combined dreams and thoughts of the all ness of the in the before the beginning, and with that knowing will in fact return to that point of incommunicable glorious and absolute wondrous oneness.

When at that point, our independence will in fact realize that there is no isolating one from the other, we will also know at that point, there never was any separation or even independence. Only that total allness of the allness that we have always been and will always be.

With this new being within me, I truly do ponder these things that I know to be truth.

For I myself in body am but the visualized and desired outcome of First beings thought, with the independent consciousness of Mind that I myself am, and now inhabit as female, woman.

When our family is at last with us, will it be as me, or will it be as my mate?

What will it be like? What will it look like? Will it have the desire to be as creative as first being, its bodily sire? Or will it be more as I am, in constant awe and contentment just to be a part of this glorious place and experience.

Male and female knew that they were in truth starting a new specie, and for them a whole different and to now untried situation. For the two of them had been free to do anything at any time anywhere.

Feeling that the time would not be to long, for as they had been watching many of the different animals and the manner in which they had to care for their young, they looked at each other with wonder.

Will we have to feed and care and watch over our newborn, as the animals seem to have to do? For sometimes as many as sixty even ninety orbits of the great giver of warmth?

Will not this new being be as we are? To play a part in what goes on within the scheme of things as a member of the family of life here on this small planet?

It will be wonderful to watch this first being in this physical dimension. In fact the first of it's kind in the specie, and to show it all that we have learned in this physical world.

As time moved by very rapidly, her body was expanding and as the new life form was growing, she was in her countenance, becoming very serene with that creative glow and independent beauty that is woman's alone to cherish and understand.

Many of the animals seemed to stay somewhat closer to her now. For it was very apparent that the moment of entering for this new being was very close.

The woman called to her mate to stay close to her.

The man and woman had in the past few months put together a wonderful and cozy warm nesting place for her to give this new life its freedom in and as a physical being. In the past the dark periods of the day would be spent in study of the stars and also for rest. Usually under or in a tree, but many times out in the vast open areas to better see some of the allness that was spread out before them at night. So a shelter hadn't been necessary. After watching the animals, they decided to prepare a dwelling. The woman had chosen first tree as the place, so they hollowed out an area from under a mighty root of first tree and there placed the bedding for the coming event. They lined it with soft grasses and fragrant flowers.

Now was the time for that process. Our beautiful lady laid down and got as comfortable as she could under the circumstances.

With her mate at her side ready and yet not emotionally prepared for whatever would come next, for neither had personally been the participant, only the observers.

Until now, only the generations of animals had been any clue as to the manor of birth. But, were they the same as the animals?

The body functions were in fact very similar, with this in mind; they personally through creative thought and the life-giving source of all things, did in mind and consciousness know what was to be. For all that was happening was only a part of their complete plan and goal.

The new life was entering the world and first man reached out to receive their newborn who was now first child.

As for the birth itself, it had now been accomplished, and he looked down upon the infant.

There was a very new feeling that seemed to overwhelm and somewhat humble him. He now knew that there was a part of this process that until now had not, at least by him, entered mind.

This woman had created within her body a duplicate of them and yet independent.

While looking at his first born, a smile came to his face. The child was still connected to the mother by his now life source.

In front of him was the likeness of himself. He looked up to his beloved and in her eyes saw a knowing twinkle that made him think somehow she knew, and was pleased.

Now again the situation hit him with the force of the first wind that tree had to withstand, as the responsibility of spreading of ones seed brings along with it.

Here in front of him was a very helpless, very little, very dependent, very loud being.

What to do? Oh, what to do? The woman sat up and leaned forward and somehow, knew what to do. Then she took the child from first man and put him to her chest with an embrace that even furthered the bonding with their child.

As the new mother started to clean the baby, the newborn seemed to instinctively and with propensities to the totally foreign act of feeding, start it's life as family.

Father is watching this seemingly very normal act of the very new and first born and never before done or seen as to this new species, yet it was.

Was this but a part of the nature of adapting to what was the beginning of survival?

The child grew very quickly, and with his clear and inquisitive mind and with the intuitive source of consciousness, which was his motivating factor. He needed no encouragement to go out and watch the wonders of nature; it was all there for him to see.

Mother and Father would sit him down and tell how all things came to be, of how the stars were in the sky, of all the plants and most certainly of the greatest of all the plants, first tree.

They told him of how the animals became a part of life here on their little planet and why they all have some of the same basic essential parts to sustain life on this world. They tried to tell of the in the before the beginning and how all things were but a part of the ONE.

As he would play with the animals he became totally involved with them and as had his fathers' the young boys life was mostly centered with his friends, the animals.

Years flew by and the boy was more as a man in stature, much as his father. His features were very soft and beautifully handsome for there was also some of his mother showing through.

His parents tried very hard to explain that his body was but the vehicle of the mind and that the mind was how and what he truly was. They tried to tell him that he was as they were, infinite in every way with a consciousness and being of the in the before.

That the body was of this earth and physical dimension, but he truly was not, that he too was a part of the allness.

All of the stories that they told him were very interesting and he very much enjoyed listening to them, but he was always in somewhat of a hurry to get back to his favorite animals, for playing with them had been a very major part of his young life.

The young man could relate to the animals and could understand what they were. He had watched them being born and how they had to survive and that their entire life was spent on staying alive and expanding the family to carry on as they had. Lovingly laying down their lives when their time was spent. This he had seen.

Almost without notice to the boy, mother was again about to have another child. Mother and Father called to their son and told him that they would soon have a new addition to the family and he a friend, and would like him to help look after the new child.

To show it all that he had learned and loved so much.

The second child was now a part of the family. There was a second son. He too was born under the mighty tree and the limitless universe above.

Mother and father looked at each other and were thinking how will we call our boys? We must give them names. Father, you name our first-born. Yes, we will call him Niac. Mother what will we call our newborn and second son? We will call him Leba.

Mom and dad had been watching Niac for several years now and could see that his relation to the animals was very strong and his understanding and knowing of their ways and life styles of survival was in fact a part of his own life.

They felt that maybe with Leba there should be more time spent

explaining his true origin. And also make sure that he did in fact understand all that had taken place to this point.

Their lessons with Leba started very early in his life. They had seen that in this world of the physical, it would be difficult to make an understanding of the non-physical and true nature of what life is and where it had originated.

It seemed to mother and father that when the new child was born there was at least some knowing and mental communication as it is with all of collective mind and the all ness of life, but as time goes by and the child gets caught up into the physical routine of life, the need for mental communication and any knowing of the non physical wanes to oblivion.

We will call first man (Moda) and first woman (Ave).

Now Moda and Ave were realizing that unless they explained all of what was truth to at least one who would carry it on and teach others about the true meaning of life and its beginning, it could be lost.

What a loss that would be. Not to be aware that you were a part of the allness of the One Mind (True Origin).

The years virtually flew by and the two sons grew and advanced in their own ways. First son, Niac continued in his love with the animals. While Leba acquired more fascination towards plant life, as Moda and Ave had kept him closer to them for a much longer time, to teach him of the creative power that was within him and of the absolute and all encompassing Source of all that there is, and what he too was a part of.

During this time of training Leba had grown very attached to the great tree for it was very close to their dwelling place.

Although Leba's features were a bit more like his father, his temperament and obvious contentment with all things as they were and his consistent times with himself as he would climb high into the great tree, gave off more of the attitude of his wonderful Mother.

The two brothers were friends but not close, for their interests were very distant in nature. Niac would spend most of his time living with nature and all the many animals that come with it, while Leba spent most of his time closer to home.

His interests were of the nature that can't be put into words, but in the area of his Father, and yes his Mother, but mostly father, for the Father had planted the seed from his mind that the mighty tree of which he loved and spent so much time had become.

First being had in fact created the physical body that his consciousness now occupied as first being.

This fact was the one thing that most interested Leba for he knew that he was born of his Mother, and his Father. Father was in fact first being, but was he Father. Was he or even could he be? Now Leba had gone with his brother Niac and watched the animals in every facet of their lives.

Leba knew and understood the functions and personal relations of the animals, for he had spent a lot of time with Niac, his brother watching them and just being with them from birth.

Watching that process, to the fullest degree and feelings through their life span as time may be seen on the physical plain.

There was always a physical joining to some degree of two distinctively separate and different parts of the same species.

Leba contemplated this as he would sit and meditate high up in Tree. To what point was Father now of this world? To what degree was Mother a part of this physical plain? To what percent was even he now a part?

Was this thing that he could see and feel and to what seemed to be the logical conclusion really him?

Am I the Being that walks this land? Am I the person that my Mother and Father have explained to me to the point of disbelief and understanding within the confines of the physical?

Father said what he had done was to create a vehicle in which the consciousness of which he is, could better understand what was taking place on this planet.

To a very similar degree that of when he too had joined with the creation in that far distant world in creative construction across the infinite cosmos, so to better relate on an individual bases what was possible in this newly formed dimension.

My Father Moda also told me that by the time he had gotten back to this planet where the seed of tree had been planted, tree had expanded somewhat of itself to nearly the size that it now stands. It had had no point of size or reason for limitation put into it before my leaving it, for the lessons I desired on the distant world as one of it's creatures.

Father said it was at that time of first seeing tree that he decided that perhaps many would be better then one mighty on this small planet.

As Leba ran these things through his mind, he began to realize that what he had been told by his Father was not something that would be easily understood as to the physical.

For Father was in fact not a physical being. He was the creative consciousness of the in the before while using the physical body as a means to better understand any and all aspects of the Life Source that is.

Mother too has told me that she is but the individualized consciousness of the in the before, occupying a physical body as a companion to Moda, my physical Father.

Mother and Father have both said WE ARE IN THIS WORLD, BUT TRULY NOT OF IT.

But Mother and Father, you are my parents of this world.

Who am I? What am I? My dearly beloved son. You are too of what we are. In the physical form you are our son Leba and also your brother Niac is our physical offspring, but that is where it ends, this physical dimension is but the outpouring of creative thought.

It is but the mirror image of a dream within the mind of the creator, and that creator is but the one that has a dream and the desire to create the reality of that dream.

You, my son, are the creator of your dreams. But Father, I do not understand. I am but flesh and blood created of your dream to become but a species in this on going of a life cycle.

What am I? Mother steps in as she had been listening to the mentally tormenting discussion between her mate Moda and Leba, her son.

Leba, my dear one. I consciously and with absolute understanding entered this body, which was in fact not total and complete. So, I too was given the opportunity to some what finish the design of this one that I Am, that I now exist in and as on this physical plain.

As for your question, who you are, my son, yes the basic mold was set. The design too, within a degree had its parameters, only as a starter mold of clay might be given you.

Within the basic fundamental minimal limitations, you within your own personal consciousness finalized the design, to meet the independent goals that you have chosen to achieve while in this one particular form or you may say individual, as our son.

You are indeed as we are. You too are of the in the before the beginning.

Your creative consciousness that is within this beautiful being standing before me is as much a part of the allness of the Infinite as your Father and I, It's just that you decided to enter into this world within the unfolded being that too was a part of my dream.

It has become apparent that to some degree there is a fundamental loss of the basics of our true being when entering this plain through the process of physical birth.

Leba went out into the far fields where he knew his brother Niac spent most of his time.

There were many species of animal there and it seemed as though Niac had chosen them all to be more as his family then his parents and brother were.

As the days, the years, had passed, Niac had of course, acquired a taste for some fruits and other varied specie of edible plant life over others and had gathered some of his favorites that he had found. Some from far distant areas and brought them to where he spent most of his time and had planted them there. He had managed to bring seeds of fruit trees, of many different types of grains and such a wonderful array of berries.

The area of this marvelous and extensive orderly garden was in itself a site to behold.

When he came upon this magnificent scene, Leba knew that Niac too must have come to the realization of the truth of his being.

What was laid out before him was most assuredly of the creative mind of infinite design.

The dwelling, the trees, the fields, with their grains and berries, the marvelous little winding stream flowing into a calm and obviously designed pond.

Woven vines supported the small but functional dwelling low in a tree, then continued to the ground and integrated itself as a part of the landscape, which went down and around the pond and out to the crest of the small hill. The many varied plants were as borders for paths that encircled and somewhat encompassed this place. The smaller berry plants, then the larger plants and flowers and on out to the fruit baring trees. Then the great forest took over.

It was in fact, the absolute of nature in a single grouping with organization and a planned outcome.

There were a few animals wondering about, but the atmosphere was not of family, with all that was in sight, there was a noticeable emptiness within the confines of this place.

Leba only wanted to tell Niac what he now felt. Some degree of understanding of, and how magnificently wonderful he felt about it, and the feeling of infinite wonder and power that was within his beck and call to use if and when he so chose.

This new and complete knowing gave Leba an outlook now that could include and yet transcend this life and physical world that seemed to be the reality of things.

Now Leba knew that the true reality was in fact not the visible one, yet they were now so tightly intertwined that in truth they were but the two halves of a whole and complete at this point of existence of independent reality within consciousness.

This step in his growth and quest for truth and it's understanding to a degree had fulfilled his personal yearning and tied the physical self and the true nature of spirit the essence of his being, inseparable.

This knowing of truth was overwhelming.

When Niac would be at the family dwelling the subject of discussion seemed to always lead to what Leba wanted to know. About that in the before. Who cares, I am here right now and that's that. So what and shut up. I don't want to hear anymore about it.

It is not a part of my life and you all are not a part of my life either. Now leave me alone with my friends and stay away.

I don't want you around, so leave me be or I will set MY family against you.

With this last outburst from Niac as he had left their family dwelling still in Leba's mind, and yet now looking out over this extensive and spectacularly beautiful creative handy work, Leba knew that he must find his brother and ask him one more time.

He must know, but seeing that he hasn't come back to the family place I must assume that Niac does not yet understand.

Why do I feel that I need to tell him? He has listened to what Mother and Father have said. He knows that only they can explain the absolute to the degree of understanding that only they could.

Now I too know and feel what they have been saying.

As Leba continued with his search for Niac, and was now a far distance from where he had found Niac's beautiful dwelling, he came over the top of a large hill and stopped short, for there in front of him was a sight he had never before seen.

It seemed to Leba that they stretched on forever. They were the largest beasts that he had ever seen. There was Niac down there in the middle of them.

Of course, Leba was not afraid, for the human emotion of fear had not yet surfaced as a part of his life.

There was nothing to fear. Especially now with this wondrous feeling and the knowing of his infinite self.

Niac, Niac, Leba called out as he was waving his arms vigorously. Niac, Niac, come over here. Niac looked over and saw Leba off in the distance beckoning him. He gave the great beast beside him a pat and started towards Leba with a bit of a smile on his face for they had not been together for many years.

Well, well, well, what brings you out this far from your beloved tree, my brother? How are Mother and Father? Are we still a specie of four or are there more now?

Leba was not prepared for Niac's words.

He was so wrapped up in his own personal excitement that he started blurting out what he wanted to tell Niac without thought of where Niac was in his own thoughts and feelings. Niac, do you hear what I am saying? Can't you understand how simple it all truly is?

I am afraid this was not the best way to try to explain his feelings, for to Niac it was no more than he would always hear when he was at home and that was the very reason that he had left.

Be gone with you Leba, be gone and now stay gone. Do not bother to find me again.

This saddened Leba to a point of tears as he ran back to ask his Mother and Father why Niac was acting as he was.

Leba's exalted feelings and need to share with his brother had been dashed into this unknown mental upheaval of sorrow and remorse.

Why wouldn't Niac ever discuss or relate his feelings to the rest of them? Why wouldn't Niac come to the family dwelling under Tree any more? Could it be that he maybe did not understand? Could it be that he had so associated himself with his animal family that the passion of survival in and of itself had in fact blocked out the memory or the conscious awareness of his natural family? Is the peace in animals not unlike the peace of the in the before?

Mother Ave saw Leba coming and went out in wonderment as to the state he was in.

What my son is this? I do not understand your condition.

Leba my son, what have you done? What is this? I do not understand these feelings and emotions that you are showing me? Tell me my son, what has happened?

Leba was nearly as baffled as his mother except that he did know the point at which this new and overwhelming emotion had erupted from deep within his soul.

This was not a desirable feeling. For it seemed to Leba that while feeling this way there was an unusual drain of the living source that was as he knew, his very being.

Was this strange new emotion destructive to this body?

Leba began to tell Mother what had gone on between his brother Niac and himself.

As he was telling the tale, Father joined them and listened in silence. As the story continued, after a while he looked into the eyes of his beloved Ave, he saw for his first time this emotion that brought tears.

For some reason the tale that was being told and this unknown and strange emotional feeling of sorrow was not only for his son Leba, but of what he also felt from within the mind of Ave.

Moda began to feel in his mind the agony that was generating this powerful emotion and within him it seemed as though his body was filling, but filling with what?

Moda allowed the pressure to continue while Leba was finishing this heart-rending tale. Moda too felt a tear in his eye and with the tear; this pressure in his gut became an ache. This too was an unknown and distressful change in his attitude.

It was as though the full cycle of emotions had taken place within the past few moments. Love, concern, compassion, and now at least for Moda, another feeling with a power intensity that had not been felt by him at least since the mental conflict on how to move the seeds.

Even as he was then, he had almost abandoned the project and gone off to that far distant world in order to acquire a more personal and direct idea for the purpose of understanding.

It was that feeling of the unknown with this new emotion of sorrow mixed with the unknown and mounting ache within, again another is developed as conflict between his two sons and with this stress.

While allowing all of these emotions to occupy his creative mind at one time, what could the outcome be?

There was no way to know for all of these emotions were new and untried, but now with all of them mixed and yet separate it was as though they all lumped into one new emotional feeling, confusion.

Now with this new overpowering emotion, as before, again another pops up, fear, and as an anguish, which comes back to distress of mind.

As Moda was churning and mixing his feelings while contemplating what was taking place, not only with his own state of mind and being, but that of Ave and Leba, let alone the son that had for some reason chosen animals company over family.

Could it be that Niac had in fact felt some or perhaps all of these emotions draining him similar as other beings.

If in fact had Niac gone through this chain of emotions, and within and of himself, was it any wonder that he had secluded himself and sought only the company of the animal kingdom as his companions.

If Niac had not found a way to discuss these feelings, and felt as though perhaps he alone had them would not the emotion of the mental anguish alone have hampered his ability to rationalize even to a stable family much less to any possible point with desire of what was in the before?

Now here was Moda contemplating in his mind the rationalization of an infinitely irrational part of being human, for every situation will be seen from the perspective of the individual and their point of view, and in fact to enhance their point even without truth.

Here stands the creator of most of what there was on this one small, yet wondrous planet excluding only the independent and of themselves infinite beings of his mate Ave and his sons Niac and Leba.

Even they were the outcome of the ongoing of the creative evolution, which had become and was now but a part of nature. For to continue there must be growth and that is life and life is of the source of the in the before the beginning of which all things are but a part of.

Ave too was having sentimental and emotional challenges with also to her an unknown result, but now with Ave this controversy within family and the outcome as emotional strain was to her perception from an altogether far distant and somewhat impersonal nature.

And yet, in fact the very closest to a woman for she alone knew that her physical body along with another individualized spiritual soul was now producing a new offspring.

Time, for some reason has a way of passing very quickly, and with that passing the hard emotions too have a way of drifting out of mind and are forgotten.

Niac and his desire to be left alone was being honored, not totally because of his desire, but with family changes taking place at a pace to where the subject of Niac was not first priority. You might say out of sight out of mind. That may sound a little less than kind, but in fact that is the way that it is to a degree.

Our newest member of the family was the most beautiful little girl on the earth. She had the disposition and distinct beauty of her mother, Ave.

As she grew, she loved being with Leba as he would take her out into the fields and explain to her the things of this world in a manor that she could understand. Leba had to some what struggle through the understanding of the physical and of the in the before from a completely different perspective, for his teachers were in fact themselves strictly and totally of the in the before and in truth could not explain from the physical side.

The total and absolute believing was what made it truth to the person who was in fact born in and as a physical being.

Leba loved to talk on these matters and would explain them until there was an understanding.

He himself was in fact learning as the conversations and explanations from his point of view would go on.

Our newest member of the human race whom we will call Manl was growing in wisdom and knowledge, for her desire to know was without comparison.

The lessons were being absorbed within her and yet she not only would learn a lesson, but also would use what she had learned in new and creative ways.

Manl had an intuitive knowing of what she was so all that was being told her was in fact just reaffirming what she already felt. With this knowing, she not only loved being up in Tree with her thoughts but of course talking with Leba and her Father and Mother.

Manl had an uncanny relationship with all the animals that she came into contact with. There was a conscious awareness between them, that knowing that they, and all things were in fact of the same and the entire ONE. With this communing between them there was a tremendous love and comforting association.

As the years flew by for Manl discovery was her prime motivator for there was nothing that was not of interest to her.

One day as Leba and Manl had ventured a much farther distance then was customary they came upon a mighty valley that was incomparably beautiful and somewhat unique in its manner and layout of plant life with unbelievable variety.

As they wandered down totally involved in the beauty and fragrance of the many types of flowers they came upon a wonderful little river. As they looked up the river towards it's source, Leba had a feeling of recognition in his mind, but what was it?

They started up a path apparently created by the animals that would come for water, but the further they went the stronger the feeling of having been there before was becoming.

Manl looked at Leba and questioned him. I do not recognize your attitude. I feel something that I do not know. What are you feeling? Why do you seem apprehensive? How could you feel anything but perfection in a place like this? Leba pondered, I at first did not recognize it, for the forest has again taken over the bigger part of it.

Our brother Niac put this place together and lived here for many years alone with only his animals and would not associate with Mother, Father and myself and I still cannot understand his reasoning.

My dear sister there is one thing I do feel here and that is when I last talked with Niac, he told us to never try to find him again or he would set his animals against us.

Manl looked over to Leba with a bit of a smile, Leba, you, Mother and Father have told me about Niac and his strange ways. From what I have heard there is nothing strange about him, only that he may look at things a little differently then you do and maybe that this very beautiful world is the place he has chosen to live and recognize.

You know Leba, as well as I, that we can leave here any time that we may choose, and that we, in fact, are here because we did choose to come and be a part of this world that Father started.

Don't you feel that it is up to each of us to perhaps create our own life and existence in a manner of our own choosing and just maybe this is not the way that you may choose yours? But surely does not make it wrong, does it?

I want to see and meet my brother. I know that if the animals love him, there is good in him and this whole thing is just a misunderstanding. I want to make it right. I will go alone if I must, but I will go.

Yes, Manl, I know. You must go and I too must go.

It has been many years now and that in itself, I feel is wrong. I do hope Niac will accept us.

Where would Niac have gone Leba was asking himself? Well Manl, we have to go to where I last saw him in a great valley far off to the north.

Manl, you must know, Niac would never listen to any of us in the area of the in the before.

Mother and Father never got into telling him the total facts and truths of his true being, for they did not realize that he would not know these things of himself and would have to be taught.

Until after I was with them and Niac was off with the animals. Teaching himself of what life is, and that would be only from a physical point and that too as the animals would relate to existing through survival.

Manl, I hope you can see what we may be facing. They moved on to the north truly hoping to find Niac in good spirits. Of course with beautiful Manl there was no doubt, but that they would be greeted with open arms and rejoicing.

With Leba there seemed to be that same degree of apprehension that had come over him in Niac's inspiring garden. For his own reasons these feelings would not leave. Of course his wishes were as Manl's, for an endearment with the brother that he never really had, but he was with Niac face to face when he had left for the last time those many years ago and was now reliving that time in his mind.

As Leba and Manl walked hand in hand, the tears began to flow over his cheeks as those memories again cut into his soul, for through the past years he within himself had been feeling the emotion of what we now call guilt.

In their last meeting, he, Leba had been so excited with his own feelings and wanting to tell them to Niac that he hadn't even said hello to his brother, but had only managed to aggravate him with his almost arrogant manner that he had figured everything out and that Niac must listen or there just wasn't any hope for him.

Leba had felt that perhaps he had been the one to drive Niac away from the family.

My, my, my, only four people on earth and all these emotions. This is the point. We are our emotions. We are what we think.

As Leba had been taking his mental journey Manl had run on up ahead anxious to see what was there, wanting to be at her goal and forgetting to enjoy the path it takes to reach it. But with good reason. This was to be a totally new experience for her.

She was going to meet another being that had a mind as hers, that could talk and feel and dream and make those dreams a reality. Someone she had never met or seen. She was excited.

Come on Leba, let's get a move on. It is growing darker. We must find a place to spend the night. Leba was so caught up in his thoughts that the darkness overtook them and he lagged far behind Manl.

As Manl ran on also in her dreams, she came on a ridge overlooking a wondrous plain. She just knew this was the place that Niac must have been when last seen by brother Leba.

For Leba had told her the story many times and had explained this very place that she now stood.

A tingling of excitement overwhelmed her and tears of joy and happiness came to her eyes. She looked out over the endless expanse of this marvelous valley. It did to some degree remind her of Niac's other area that he had abandoned, for it was to him far to close to the human family.

Of course, Manl did not know if in fact this was where Niac had made his new dwelling, but as she was listening to the sounds of the animals and the birds, she saw a small fire down at the base of the ridge she was on and some distance off to her left.

Without thought she quickly headed for it, not thinking of Leba or the darkness or of any situation that could confront her. She had a focused goal and was determined to see Niac.

As she ran down the path the sounds of animal seemed to be closing in on her. Of course there was no fear, for she knew that she and the animals were as one.

She had never known anything but love with all animals and their sounds were to her friendly and comforting. Companionship to help guide her on this quest.

She continued to run down the path. She knew that the light had to be quite close. Her heart was pounding, not only from the running, but even more so of the excitement and of the unknown that she was dashing headlong into.

The path ran under a giant and mighty tree with branches that draped not only to the ground but seemed to extend almost to the stars. As Manl ran under a large branch, a massive and powerful arm reached down and grabbed her just as a very large and savage beast leaped for her with all intent to continue with its own survival.

Leba, how did you? She somewhat yelled as being swept up out of harms way. As she was turning to face him she knew to her very soul this was not Leba. Then to her conscious mind the reality of what had just happened burst out with mixed emotions. Some of which Manl was uncertain of.

Excitement was what she had been running on for the past several days of their journey and quest in search of Niac.

The tantalizing new emotion of the unknown that too had sprung up with some real situations was for some reason right now mixing with a feeling she had never before encountered, being in the mental state within this extremely fast moving and for the first time life threatening situation, we will have to say it fringed on another unknown, fear.

Now face to face with Niac, all of her lives situations, the trials of her lessons with Leba for the understanding of the truth of her being, and all the whys, deluged into Manl's mind.

All this along with the stories of Niac and the uncertainties of what he might do and what his reactions would be.

This all happening within a very few seconds period of time, overwhelmed her into a state of mental shutdown.

While Leba had been mentally re-examining his life here on this physical plain, the continuation for survival within the animal kingdom had not slowed and since the hungry beast had missed out on a sure meal, it would be continuing with it's search for substance. To the animal it was survival of the species more then of the individual but it was always to survive.

The beautiful great beast moved as though it were walking on air. It made no sound. It's ears and eyes were at their peak.

There before it on the path walked Leba totally wrapped up in his world of dreams.

With Leba's knowing and understanding of the One Infinite Mind, you might say, why didn't he realize this possible up coming tragedy?

We also know now that we create the life and situations that we are in and Leba had allowed himself to become so involved with his dream of the past in his mind that he had in fact shut off his conscious mind of the here and now. The things that were happening and about to happen were not a part of his reality.

To the beast, Leba was in fact the only reality and focus of his here and now. With a mighty leap he landed squarely on Leba's back, his saber-sized claws riddling into and tearing apart Leba's magnificent and perfect physical body. The beast easily and mercifully with absolute precision and uncanny speed ended Leba's physical stay in this as yet very strange encounter with life.

Leba was jolted back to the reality of the now situation which had just unfolded. What has happened? Where? How? Who is that down there? Where am I? What is that ripped and torn creature down there on the ground?

That great beast has just taken that thing for food. Why am I up here looking down on everything?

Is that my body? Yes, yes it is, and I am again back to my infinite self as of the in the before the beginning of this stay.

Wow!

Manl was being carried very gently down the tree by Niac as her consciousness returned. She now realized that even though Niac had been totally without human companionship and completely integrated within this animal life style of survival, there were those qualities of gentleness that are inherent within all life.

Who are you? Where do you come from? Why are you here? Are you Niac? But of course you are. I am Manl and Leba is back on the trail coming with me to find you.

All color and emotion completely and instantly drained from Niac's countenance.

Niac knelt to the ground and gently placed Manl on the fallen leaves.

Leba, Leba, why did you come to find me? You know nothing of the true nature of survival with the animals.

Where is he now? Niac barked out. Where is he? As he jumped to his feet, on the run, he looked back.

Climb that tree. Climb it to the very top. Do it now. Niac vanished from site in the darkness and trees.

Niac knew there was a very strong chance that the animal would find Leba, for it was their time for hunting and there was nothing that would or even could stop its sole purpose.

As Niac ran back up the path, he could also hear the animals, but to him he knew there was a time for all things and this was the time for feeding with a lot of the larger beast.

He also respected their nature and ways of surviving for it was their way. To Niac this too was his way to a large extent as it was as he had been for most of his span on this plain.

Niac came over the crest of the hill and there lay Leba, ripped and torn beyond recognition.

There were no animals or anything of any nature even close to Leba's body. As Niac stepped closer to Leba, he stopped short, for there was such a concentrated consciousness of contemplation surrounding Leba that it literally brought Niac to his knees.

What is this power? Is this not but the shattered body of my own brother Leba?

As Niac knelt there a few minutes, the force seemed more to engulf him than to repel as at first and Niac could feel a presence, but what was this feeling? Or was it just a feeling? Was this the life force and source of Leba's true being that he so wanted to tell me of? Was this non-physical power and force Leba's true being of in the before?

Niac reached out and picked up Leba's body with no resistance or negative feelings of any kind. In fact, he had a feeling of closeness that he had never before sensed.

As he stood to his feet, he raised his brother's body up over his head. With all the emotional build-up exploding in his mind, let out a shout that had to penetrate the very soul of the Infinite allness.

For the first time in his life as a physical being, he was feeling the emotion of love, without being able to receive it or in fact even give it. For that is the only true nature of love. Unconditional.

Niac knew Leba was no longer with the body, but he held him close to himself and tears came to his eyes. Niac did not understand what this was, but he did know and could feel a loss within. He knew that Leba would not return.

Niac headed back for the great tree and that other human that had burst into his life and was now waiting his return.

It was getting towards morning by now and just a hint of gold was far off on the horizon.

But coming up at the far side of the great valley were some of the largest and darkest clouds that had as of yet ever appeared in the skies of this small and somewhat peaceful world.

Moda and Ave knew that Leba and Manl had left many days before but this in itself was not unusual for in fact, to the two of them time was not a factor in their lives.

Moda had been on this planet for many thousands of generations. He had been very involved in the creative evolution of the plant and the animal in their on going of survival.

Moda himself as a being was not of the physical except as the creative manifestation of thought within this now physical dimension.

Ave too, was a manifestation of both Moda and finally her own creative thought. So she too did not deal with time as a reality. For the two of them, it was but a day-by-day experience to learn from with no real thought of what was to come.

As for Niac, Leba, and Manl, the bodies that they occupied, had gone through somewhat of an evolution in their own right while developing an unfolding within its own individual way, but they (body) were more of the physical world.

Niac was coming up on the great tree of the valley where he had left Manl. He too was in deep thought as he was carrying Leba's lifeless form.

From far up in the tree Manl could see Niac coming. What was that he was carrying? Was it an anim---al? No, it was her adoring brother Leba.

Manl frantically started down the tree. As she was descending her mind was racing. What? What was this? Why was Leba so, so?

Manl loved all the animals that she had ever seen and they too had loved her. She had never truly been with the roaming beast of the open fields and seen their ways of survival, such as large beast taking down smaller and on down the chain so to exist.

The thought that an animal would have done such a thing was not only incomprehensible, that fact would have not even have entered Manl's mind.

With the sparse information and very negative outlook as to the character of Niac, the thought and reality of this type was within the realm of possibilities, even though the understanding of what is called death was still not within the consciousness of the human mind except perhaps to that point within the extent understood by Niac as to survival within the animal kingdom.

As for Manl, she was taking this in a very personal way for her loving brother Leba was very obviously lifeless and without conscious ability to function on his own.

Not knowing the situation and circumstances surrounding this apparent savage outburst, prejudged by Manl as the doings of Niac, which he had in fact warned them of, if anyone of them came into what he might consider his territory.

Manl without considering any other possibilities, only the fact that in her mind and degree of understanding this seemingly disastrous and emotional situation was caused by Niac.

As Niac was coming closer to the tree and Manl, he dropped his head and again raised Leba high into the air and with a somewhat garbled and emotion filled voice called his brothers name. Leba, Leba.

To Manl, this conduct seemed to be an act of triumph over Leba and what he believed. With all that was so very quickly rushing through her mind a very chilling and mentally disturbing emotion froze her for an instant.

To us, this emotion is known all too well as fear and is very body and mind crippling. It will render our minds into a prejudged conclusion and our bodies into a rigid state and non-cooperating mode.

Manl's reaction to this new and very strange and unbelievably powerful emotion seemed to push her consciousness of unconditional love and infinite secure ness to that of the animal and the physical need of survival.

Had all of Manl's beliefs been abolished and discarded in an instant of an unknown emotion? Or were they more like the animals then was realized when in the physical form? For whatever truth that may deem true the reaction from the emotion stood firm.

Now as Manl, much slower, continued down the tree she moved around to the backside, then scurried to a point to where she could no longer hold back and jumped to the ground. The instant she touched the earth she was headed for Father and Mother and the only real safety that she could count on in her mind within the rapid manner of the entire unfolding drama.

Not understanding Manl's mindset, Niac stopped short in bewilderment. Who was this being? Why was she here? Why was she running away? Where was she going? Had she not come with Leba? Did she not care to know about Leba?

Manl ran as fast as she could to get away from an unwanted situation and the possibility of other unforeseen problems with Niac.

Manl felt she must find her Mother and Father to let them know what she thought had happened and her concern of what Niac might do.

Niac started back up the path, headed to where he knew the family dwelling was when he was last there at the base of first tree.

Manl knew she was a very long distance from her home and parents and now being alone with this terrible energy draining emotion of fear within her mind and now situation possibilities whirling her almost to dizziness.

The desire of the unknown that had pushed her ever faster to Niac now had reversed from it's stimulating excitement to a tearful and fearful mind and body draining want to escape from Niac.

With every hurried step, Manl's mind spun her ever further into the abstract reality of what she perceived as truth.

In the condition of her thinking processes there was negativity piling upon negativity which only reinforced the strangle hold of fear, which had taken hold of her ever tighter and could only enhance and propel the fright and horror of but a partial truth as to cause.

Moda and Ave could feel a disturbance within the vibrations of consciousness, but without having had to participate in the physical plain as a product of or having truly been a physical being, could only sense the emotions through mind, but without having witnessed the incident or have had such an emotional episode, did not realize the magnitude of what had happened within the realm of the human species.

The first human as a physical being, had died.

Manl ran up to the home dwelling in such a state of mental disorder and near physical collapse that there was no way to read or make sense of her condition.

Moda walked from behind the dwelling and seeing Manl's physical condition ran to meet her. She was nearly covered with dirt being held on by blood from the cuts she got from running through the tree branches and under brush.

Niac with his long stride and phenomenal strength and with using the path was not all that far behind Manl. As Manl was running up to her Father, Niac was heading out of his first habitat that was only a few hours distance.

Father, Father, she cried as she threw her arms around him sobbing in complete hysterias.

Manl my dear little one, why? What? What can I do? Mother was coming out the doorway now and seeing Manl ran over to them pulling Manl to her breast and holding her tightly with a concerned eye toward Moda. Both of them remembered the last time such emotional feelings had come home. What is it my dear one? What is the cause of this trembling? What can I do?

Niac, Mother. Father, it was Niac. A very old but familiar lump came into Moda's chest. A very unfamiliar but remembered emotional feeling renewed its mental clamp upon his mind.

Niac, what? I am not sure but Leba is no longer with his body and I saw Niac carrying it torn and mangled. Niac tore my beloved brother Leba to a point beyond that of life. I saw him limp and lifeless in Niac's arms.

Manl went on with her story, as she perceived that it had happened. Sobbing with every word and shaking with fear as she looked back down the path.

Moda listened to the heart-rending tale from his limp and still sobbing beloved daughter, along with the old story of his now lifeless son Leba.

He was emotionally creating a drama within his mind that was putting Niac in a position never before assumed by anything. His place was now within the created circumstances of a creative mind that was also experiencing the most devastating of all emotions. Anger.

Within Moda's mind, he was trying to rationalize what he was picturing, and questioning the very basics of all that had come to be, and all from but a thought.

Moda looked back over his shoulder and there coming up the path with the lifeless form of Leba in his arms was Niac.

There was next to an explosion within Moda's mind. As he slowly turned toward Niac, he raised his arms into the air and his entire body seemed to extend out and a shadow began to block the very light on Niac's path.

With very mixed troublesome and confusing untried emotions, Moda within his very creative and personal reasoning spoke the words. Let it be gone. All of it. Let it be gone.

Everything that had come on this planet as from the physical instantly disappeared. The planet was bared to the lifeless dirt of the original sphere.

Moda stood there. Beside him stood Ave and close by was Tree as tall and full of life as ever.

Also beside him and Ave were two powerful and radiant balls of energy floating in mid air. One was at the very spot where Manl had been. The other was close to the three of them. Also down where Niac had been, was another.

The allness of the allness. Every stitch of creative thought had stopped.

Thought itself was as though in a vacuumed container and sealed tight.

No, thought had not stopped. Only creative thought, collective contemplation was of what had and was happening on a very small and seemingly insignificant and again nearly barren rock.

Was this physical dimension worth what it was seeming to bring? Even to that part which was merely an observer from participant to even on the infinite scale.

Were these human emotions so strong and destructive that they could control a mind to the point of taking the beauty and life of an entire plant and strip it all away in but one unguarded thought from it's Creator?

What of the physical human and its independently creative mind that also seem to be but a tangle of nerves and a bombshell of emotions.

Was this obliteration of ones total creation the outcome when an independent and individual creator has total and complete control and say, of all that there is? Can it be ended upon a whim and even from a wrongly perceived situation?

The independent sphere of energy that was with the group began to move towards the one that was now where Niac had been. As it moved very close, communication of mind again began.

Niac, my brother in the physical and still my brother in the spirit. We are again as one. The understanding is now with us. The veil that seemed to block our minds has been lifted.

We can again comprehend our place within the Infinite. This past experience has taught me while as Leba, that when at times one might not remember their true place, as a part of the Infinite, one must not forget that we all are a part of each other.

Leba and Niac's Infinite life presences began to move closer to Manl, Moda, and Ave.

All heard the communication that had taken place, and now being back within their normal form all thought and understanding of what had taken place was now as an instant replay within mind.

Moda began to speak. There was not so much as a fleeting thought to escape from a single soul.

All of Infinite and Creative Mind did in fact want to know Moda's feelings from the physical side of the action he had taken upon seeing Niac coming up the path and without any contact with Infinite Mind, how he had reacted to a situation from within human parameters and emotions, plus the lacking of truth.

I have ended all things that have seemed to come from the physical and or as a second generation. I can feel the blessing of creating and the nearly overwhelming responsibility of doing so.

There must be in this physical dimension a tremendous degree of conscious awareness in and of all things that one may think.

For unlike the in the before, where all things were created with an absolute and total in design and reason, anything but Infinite could not even be understood, but within this physical plain the forms change in design and reason as they evolve in an on-going struggle to survive as an individual and a specie.

I now have withdrawn anything that could in any way be misconstrued as a power source to any created thing. I as myself may continue as the being that I am now or I may not.

I can now see that this dimension is, as to now, the one most valuable training area that has ever been collectively produced. For it in fact puts an individual soul at a point of the absolute impersonal mental control.

The interaction with all other life forms whether in its' own specie or any other life form will in fact affect all consciousness in and of all plains of existence.

There is only one Consciousness. There is but one Life Source. All things that are, are of that One.

Niac and Leba had now joined with Moda, Ave, and Manl. Leba began to reappear as the physical being he once was. This time he was creating himself, as Moda and Ave had.

I as Leba do believe that this dimension is of the most beautiful in nature. Even though we may as that physical being not remember or in any conscious way know that we are in fact infinite.

The control and use of the mentally stimulating emotions that came, does again remind one of the importance of ones self, and the continuity of life as collective. For as the fear and sometimes feeling of aloneness comes over ones self, within the innermost point of awareness, there is a knowing.

Even though I did at many times misinterpret the feeling as perhaps self pity, I now know it was my true being trying to contact the consciousness of my physical mind.

I would beat it away with a club of self-assurances, as I was sure that I had in fact learned all truth, for I had not realized that I was, in and as myself a part of the Infinite allness of Creative Source.

Do you Moda understand now what the truth is as with Niac and this situation that was given you?

I see now that the circumstances and events leading to this moment were but emotional trials for each and every one of us from a different point of understanding. I see now that the lesson we have learned will in fact enhance all of Infinite mind as to the totality and realization of the power of emotion within the physical dimension.

Niac's physical form was now materializing next to Leba. He then began to speak. I have separated myself from my physical family for all these many generations because of a very foolish lack of understanding as to my own reasoning within the total and absolute power within the physical of what I see now as human mind. We are dominated, controlled, harassed, cared for, then rebuffed, loved and hated. All through the emotions that are produced in and as that mind within the realm of choice. Moda, without thinking, had reacted through an emotional burst.

The human being as I see it, is but a training ground for the better understanding of mind and it's by products, EMOTIONS.

Niac and Leba were again as they had been, except now THEY were the creators of their own bodies. There was no point of any control of any kind within their being, but what they themselves had created.

Manl now too had joined them again on this physical plain. By re-entering the physical, the characteristics also returned. As she came closer to Niac and Leba, there were tears in her eyes and now they were tears of never before felt joy and love.

Now an even greater thrill for she had two brothers as she was again within the consciousness of the physical. Her brief time back within the allness of Mind had re-established the greatest of all knowing, the fact of Yes I Am a part of that allness.

I cannot be eliminated, forced, or in any way coerced into anything without the absolute consent of the I that I AM.

Manl put her arms around both of her brothers and pulled their heads down to hers and they all three wept in joy.

They raised their heads and all turned to Moda. Manl began to speak. Father, what was created and has evolved upon this place, and within the short time I have spent here, I too can see the limitless advantage through the understanding of personal control within the world of emotion.

Perhaps other worlds may not want or need this entrapment of ones individual and absolute surrender of soul and essence of their being, so perhaps this could be that place to enrich the Infinite Soul by better understanding ones self as an emotional being for at least a short period of time.

I believe that this could be the one place that the Infinite all ness as individual consciousness will become a more understanding being as they move on to other worlds and creations within and beyond the physical.

By this time the consciousness and interest was building not only within this group, but as Manl looked up, the entire area was filled. There were countless radiant energy spheres ready and willing to enter the world of emotion within the physical plain.

This planet had been watched and its on-going contemplated through all of Infinite Mind and the good by far outweighed the negative, but of course within the area of training there is no negative, there is only training.

As Manl continued, it became more a discussion in mind as the newly arrived beings were joining in.

We will collectively refurbish this planet. Perhaps even better, for we are again creating, and this will be a place that all of

Creative individual source can inhabit at one time or another and will never again be under control of anything.

The individual consciousness of each and every being manifesting upon this planet will know in advance that all of the reality of this place is but an illusion created within the mind of that individual for the betterment of the self, and the Infinite knowing of all. For some. The choice may be not to experience to this degree.

At this point of the discussion there could be heard a rumbling that was so intense that it was not only heard, it was felt.

Then there was such a display of the awesome might of lightning.

To all, it was as though they were again witnessing the molding and forging of this physical dimension as their collective consciousness then had created that which was inconceivable.

So again it was beginning. First tree was standing there as majestic as it always had. Only this time the on going of plant life as trees and all the varied forms within the plant world were again spreading across the lands without seed from tree.

All the many unnumbered souls that had assembled were joining in with the glorious reconstruction of this exciting new classroom. For some it would be the first manifestation within the physical dimension. For others they would be bringing concepts from other far distant areas of unlimited space and its' infinite numbers of varied creative choices.

As the individualized entities began to manifest, they came somewhat in an orderly fashion. One or two would come at a time, for their mold was to a degree and from the point of human form the original five were the prototype.

More and more came and there were obvious variations in shape, size and color. This only enhanced the probability of total individualism even to the point of ones appearance.

As the beings were gathering and increasing in number, they began to move out over the land and it was as though the plant life was spreading out in all directions ahead of them to inhabit.

The manifesting of the human form was so much in the forefront, that the animals that were again beginning to dot the landscape were hardly noticed.

But now, why and from what source were the animals being created? When Moda first created the animal kingdom, it was as the first in all things; create from an idea and move on with and as creative evolution.

This was not necessarily to improve, but to change for more diverse and challenging opportunities for creator and created for whatever reason.

Now the animals were taking on more of an independent nature. Could this new breed of the original in fact be, perhaps entities of the same group as the others only these had decided to take on this some what less active part as to the participation within the flooding and some time tidal wave of emotion shown by the human mind?

Could it be possible that this group had taken up the position of observation instead of participation for but a short time? The parameters as from Moda's originals were not to very pleasant. Could that in fact be the reason for a choice of this kind? Knowing that the stay as this form would be relative to the creature chosen, from the one day moth to the great and mighty creatures that could span perhaps centuries?

Were they but a part of an evolution of learning? Or could it be just that point in the training needed or chosen?

Are these considerations worthy of thought? I may say this in the form of a question, but.

Moda and Ave walked over to the base of Tree and started reminiscing of their stay so far on this planet and the physical dimension in general.

Ave, I feel as though I must go back and without any personal thought re-establish within my own thought patterns that Oneness of the Allness that I have seemed to allow to drift to the side instead of at my center, as of course it always is, but I have tried to step around it.

I must come back. I shall come back as a being born into this world. For as to now we have not in truth experienced the physical life.

Yes Moda, I too have allowed my individual self to get into the way of my judgment of reason, for at times it was as though I were alone in mind and body. I can only imagine the misunderstanding of one without the absolute of knowing.

Knowledge is but understanding.

I do not know when I may come back, and then as a child of my children, but I now can see that I too must return. I have seen and to a degree felt, the emotions of these physical beings.

There is without any doubt a training and learning process that takes place here that cannot be duplicated, nor would it be needed for it is undoubtedly the most severe of all classes as it seems nearly all memory of ones true being is stripped away during or at least within a short period of time after entering this place.

I, for myself, must understand this better, or at least try, but first I too shall return within the smooth and all knowing Infinite body of the All ness of Mind.

This time the masses of self created beings who were again reproducing the species, the human race, were also very busy discussing plans and strategies within mind for mental communication was all that was known and the distances between some gatherings were substantial but there was very much a collective agreement.

One of which was, there would be for the first time an end for the class, not to say that there was a specific day of departure, but rather that each individual consciousness of the before knew it was time to leave even though not on a conscious level. It would happen for it was finished.

Now as for an amount of time that any one entity may deem necessary, needed or even desired would be the choice of that being, for time was infinite for all, and all are Infinite.

Niac, Leba, and Manl each took a partner, and again set out to understand better the nuances of the physical, mental and spiritual world.

In the beginning........**God?**.....

Comments, remarks and observations

Comments, remarks and observations

Is this the end of the story?

Never can or will there be an ending,

I do truly believe that the suffering, anguish and pain will in deed end, but the play goes on.

At least try and smile most of the time as your part will be logged into the book of life and closed never to be forgotten.

God bless you and keep you all the days of your lives as you are known and loved more then can be written.

With Love
Ken the Carpenter